Journal of Organizational Computing and Electronic Commerce

Editor-in-Chief
Andrew B. Whinston
University of Texas at Austin

Editors

Lynda M. Applegate
Harvard Business School

Ravi Kalakota
Georgia State University

Clyde W. Holsapple
University of Kentucky

Franz J. Radermacher
Universitat Ulm, Germany

Associate Editors

Jack Baroudi
New York University

Anitesh Barua
University of Texas at Austin

Erik Brynjolfsson
Massachusetts Institute of Technology

Ai-Mei Chang
National Defense University

Su-Shing Chen
University of North Carolina

Chee Ching
AT&T

Brian dos Santos
University of Louisville

Omar El Sawy
University of Southern California

Douglas Engelbart
Stanford University

David Goldstein
Boston University

John Henderson
Boston University

George Huber
University of Texas

Starr Roxanne Hiltz
New Jersey Institute of Technology

Mathias Jarke
RWTH Aachen, Germany

Rowbert Johansen
Institute of the Future

Chris Kemerer
University of Pittsburgh

John King
University of California, Irvine

Jae Kyu Lee
KAIST, Korea

Tom Malone
Massachusetts Institute of Technology

Richard Mason
Southern Methodist University

Jim McKenney
Harvard Business School

Haim Mendelson
Stanford University

Tridas Mukhopadhyay
Carnegie Mellon University

James Navarro
Hewlett-Packard Company

Gary Olson
University of Michigan

Judith Olson
University of Michigan

Ray Panko
University of Hawaii

William Richmond
George Mason University

Murray Turoff
New Jersey Institute of Technology

Kazuo Watabe
University of Shizuoka, Japan

Production Editor: Judy Ann Levine, *Lawrence Erlbaum Associates, Inc.*

Journal of Organizational Computing and Electronic Commerce is published quarterly by Lawrence Erlbaum Associates, Inc., 10 Industrial Avenue, Mahwah, NJ 07430–2262. Subscriptions for Volume 11, 2001 are available only on a calendar-year basis.

This journal is abstracted or indexed in *Computer Abstracts, INSPEC,* and *ISI: Science Citation Index, Science Citation Index Expanded, SciSearch, Web of Science, Research Alert, ISI Alerting Services, CompuMath Citation Index, Current Contents/Engineering, Computing & Technology.* Microform copies of this journal are available through Bell & Howell Information and Learning

First published 2001 by Lawrence Erlbaum Associates, Inc.

Published 2019 by Routledge
2 Park Square, Milton Park, Abingdon, Oxon OX14 4RN
52 Vanderbilt Avenue, New York, NY 10017

Routledge is an imprint of the Taylor & Francis Group, an informa business

Copyright © 2001 Taylor & Francis

All rights reserved. No part of this book may be reprinted or reproduced or utilised in any form or by any electronic, mechanical, or other means, now known or hereafter invented, including photocopying and recording, or in any information storage or retrieval system, without permission in writing from the publishers.

Notice:
Product or corporate names may be trademarks or registered trademarks, and are used only for identification and explanation without intent to infringe.

ISBN 13: 978-0-8058-9705-0 (pbk)
ISSN 1054–1721.

JOURNAL OF ORGANIZATIONAL COMPUTING AND ELECTRONIC COMMERCE

SPECIAL ISSUE

Organizational Learning and Knowledge Management

Guest Editors
James Y. L. Thong, Patrick Y. K. Chau, and Kar Yan Tam

CONTENTS

Introduction to the Special Issue on Organizational Learning and Knowledge Management 153
James Y. L. Thong, Patrick Y. K. Chau, and Kar Yan Tam

A Conceptual Model for Virtual Organizational Learning 155
Fu-ren Lin and Sheng-cheng Lin

Knowledge Sharing Through Intranet-Based Learning: A Case Study of an Online Learning Center 179
Shan L. Pan, Ming-Huei Hsieh, and Helen Chen

Internet Diffusion in Creative Micro-Businesses: Identifying Change Agent Characteristics As Critical Success Factors 197
Pascale de Berranger, David Tucker, and Laurie Jones

Introduction to the Special Issue on Organizational Learning and Knowledge Management

James Y. L. Thong
Department of Information and Systems Management
Hong Kong University of Science and Technology

Patrick Y. K. Chau
School of Business
University of Hong Kong

Kar Yan Tam
Department of Information and Systems Management
Hong Kong University of Science and Technology

This issue is based on three outstanding articles presented at the Fourth Pacific Asia Conference on Information Systems held in Hong Kong from June 1 through 3, 2000. The articles are concerned with various knowledge management issues in the Internet era. To meet the quality of this journal, expanded versions of the conference articles went through two additional rounds of review by at least three reviewers each. We thank the authors for their perseverance and the reviewers for contributing their valuable time in reviewing the articles within an expedited time frame.

The first article, "A Conceptual Model for Virtual Organizational Learning" by Fu-ren Lin and Sheng-cheng Lin, analyzes knowledge processing in virtual organizations. The authors aim to develop insights about learning in virtual organizations and propose a conceptual model for virtual organizational learning (VOL). The VOL model is illustrated through a case study involving a teachers' community that creates knowledge, shares knowledge, and forms virtual organizations across schools' boundaries.

The second article, "Knowledge Sharing Through Intranet-Based Learning: A Case Study of an Online Learning Center" by Shan L. Pan, Ming-Huei Hsieh, and Helen Chen, addresses the management of knowledge in the Internet era. Through an exploratory case study, the authors argue that successful knowledge sharing is dependent not only on the use of particular information technologies, but also on the successful creation of a knowledge-sharing environment with a knowl-

---

Correspondence and requests for reprints should be sent to James Y. L. Thong, Department of Information and Systems Management, Hong Kong University of Science and Technology, Clear Water Bay, Kowloon, Hong Kong. E-mail: jthong@ust.hk

edge-management focused Human Resource Management as the coordinator of related activities.

The third article, "Internet Diffusion in Creative Micro-Businesses: Identifying Change Agent Characteristics As Critical Success Factors" by Pascale de Berranger, David Tucker, and Laurie Jones, investigates the diffusion of Internet technology among micro-businesses—very small businesses—in the creative industry. Based on interviews with eight micro-businesses, and using Everett Rogers's innovation diffusion process as the interpretive framework, the authors identify the vital roles played by knowledge providers as facilitating change agents, including infusion into the local community, provision of customized training programs, and possession of certain unique characteristics.

A Conceptual Model for Virtual Organizational Learning

Fu-ren Lin
Sheng-cheng Lin
Department of Information Management
Application Division of the Computer and Network Center
National Sun Yat-sen University

As a trend toward virtual organizations (VOs) emerges in the era of electronic commerce, an understanding of knowledge processing is essential to sustain performance. Active learning is the key to achieving flexibility in a VO; however, few studies have focused on this dimension. In this article we attempt to assemble insights about learning in a VO by developing a conceptual model for virtual organizational learning (VOL). The VOL model is focused on transactive memory, which is composed of knowledge maps, social networks, and mnemonic functions. The initialization of modeling learning in VOs in this article has been erecting the foundation for transactive memory systems in a cyber community. A case study, Smart Creative Teachers Network, is used for demonstrating the transactive memory system for a teacher community to share and create knowledge and form VOs across school boundaries.

---

virtual organization, organizational learning, organizational memory, transactive memory, knowledge map, social network, cyber community

---

1. INTRODUCTION

Several interorganizational cooperation forms, such as strategic alliance, joint venture, and virtual organization (VO), are used to quickly share business assets to capture business opportunities. The strategic alliance defines the management framework for the joint activities of the partners based on arms-length contracts to reach a common objective. In a typical alliance, organizations may share resources and expertise to develop new products, achieve larger economic scale, or gain access to new markets or technology. In contract, the joint venture is a more formal alliance between the parties to create a legal entity to share capital, technology, and human

---

We thank the Bureau of Education of Kaohsiung City Government and Kaohsiung Municipal Huashan Primary School for their financial sponsorship, and many school teachers across Taiwan for their contributions to the SCTNet activities. We also thank the reviewers for their help.

Correspondence and requests for reprints should be sent to Fu-ren Lin, Department of Information Management, National Sun Yat-sen University, Kaohsiung City, 804, Taiwan. E-mail: frlin@cc.nsysu.edu.tw

resources, and then to pursue the shared objectives of the parent organizations. A VO is a new organizational model that uses technology to dynamically link people, assets, and ideas. A VO is an opportunity-pulled and opportunity-defined integration of core competencies distributed among a number of real organizations. A VO is the ultimate in adaptability [1].

The virtual organizational structure exhibits several advantages [2], such as

1. *Agility of a small company:* There are fewer levels of bureaucracy that allows the interfirm alliance to react more quickly. Also, these firms will be more specialized to a particular task.
2. *Resources of a large company:* The resources available to a firm working as a partner in a VO may be greater than the sum of the resources of the partner firms.
3. *Concentration on partners' core competences:* VO partnerships will be able to have improved efficiency and effectiveness through firm specialization. This specialization may result in a synergistic situation where the overall alliance has much better performance than the sum of the individual partner's separate performances.
4. *Ability to globalize:* Firms that want to take advantage of a global market opportunity can ally themselves with a firm that has expertise or market share in a given region or country.

As we enter the 21st century, a knowledge economy era, an organization's competitive advantage lies in the excellence of its learning capability. Organizations should learn to be agile to thrive in an environment with continually and unpredictably changing market opportunities. Agility can be defined in four dimensions: *efficiency, flexibility, robustness,* and *adaptation,* which denote the merits of a VO [3]. VOs focus on identifying critical core competencies in which they must maintain world-class skills to succeed, and they will acquire ancillary core competencies as needed from partners. Core competencies are the tangible, value-added activities that distinguish one company from its competitors and provide access to a variety of markets and opportunities [4]. In fact, each member of the VO is chosen because it brings something unique that is needed to meet a customer opportunity. Questions frequently asked are how physically distributed and complementary competencies can remain dispersed in a VO and still be synergised into a coherent productive resource, and how to link core competencies quickly and concurrently in a VO. Other issues such as trust, social attitudes, and organizational norms are often faced in dealing with the formation of VOs and information sharing [5, 6].

During the interaction between organizations, each organization is seeking knowledge, which can be classified into two types: *compatibility* and *complementarity,* from partner organizations [7]. Organizations seek additional knowledge in the same domain in which they have the prior knowledge. It requires absorptive capability in which prior knowledge permits the assimilation and exploitation of new knowledge [8]. On the other hand, organizations may seek knowledge in a complementary area, and thus, imply synergy of diverse resources [9]. Therefore, we can identify the two knowledge linkages between participants of a VO as compatible and complementary knowledge bases. This classification will

VIRTUAL ORGANIZATIONAL LEARNING 157

Table 1
Selective Literatures of Studying Memory and Learning

	Level			Interorganization		
Topic	Individual	Group	Organization	Joint Venture	Strategic Alliance	Virtual Organization
Memory	[13, 50]	[50–53]	[14, 54–58]	na	na	na
Learning	[10, 23, 24, 26, 59–62]	[63–67]	[10, 22, 23, 25, 62, 68–81]	[7, 82–89]	[5, 90–93, 95–103]	12

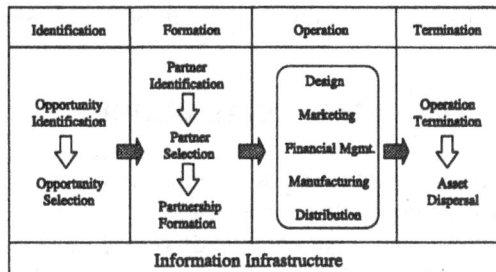

Figure 1. The life cycle of a virtual organization [2].

reflect knowledge transformation between different organizations during the virtual organizational learning (VOL) process.

Organizations must create an environment for thinking and learning to succeed as an agile competitor, and memory is necessary to organizational learning [1, 10]. However, a literature search targeting interorganizational memory and learning located very few references focusing on VO as shown in Table 1. Table 1 lists the references in organizational learning and memory based on four dimensions of ontology: *individual, group, organization,* and *interorganization*. From Table 1, we can find that all works in the interorganization dimension focus on joint ventures and strategic alliances. From VO to joint venture, the incentive to take risks decreases, the ability to settle conflicts and coordinate activities increases, and the degree of centralization increases [11]. Besides, the life cycle, number of participants, and the role of information technology (IT) in VOs are different from the other two interorganization forms. Steil et al. [12] identified the potential barriers for learning in VOs, and presented strategies for overcoming such difficulties. A more detailed insight into VOL is required. Therefore, this research aims to develop a model to describe memory and learning in a VO.

The life cycle of a VO goes through four distinct phases (*identification, formation, operation,* and *termination*), as shown in Figure 1 [2]. The identification phase involves opportunity identification, evaluation, and selection. The formation phase includes the major decision processes of partner identification, evaluation and selection, and partnership formation. The operation phase generally involves five different major decision processes including design, marketing, financial management, production, and distribution. The termination phase includes operation termination and asset dispersal. The learning across these life phases may demonstrate different learning modes and require different learning supports. The proposed VOL model should not only cover the memory and learning model for a VO, but also describe the learning process across these four life phases.

In summary, VOs are agile, and a learning environment is necessary for agile competitiveness; therefore, in this article we propose a virtual organizational model to illustrate the knowledge transference across individual, organization, and interorganization with compatible and complement any knowledge throughout the life cycle of VOs. The structure of this article is described as follows: In understanding the various organizational learning processes for the references of the VOL model, we elaborate theories of organizational memory and learning in Sections 2 and 3, respectively. We propose a VOL model in Section 4, and illustrate its applications on a cyber community in Section 5. We conclude this article in Section 6.

2. ORGANIZATIONAL MEMORY

The role of memory is interconnected with learning. Learning has more to do with acquisition, whereas memory has more to do with retention of whatever is acquired; and what we already have in our memory affects what we learn, and what we learn affects our memory. The optimal return of learning is knowledge creation. We describe memory in this section, and we describe learning related issues in the next section. We introduce individual, organization memories in their representations, meaning structures, and mnemonic functions, and then propose the virtual organizational memory. Individual memory consists of *declarative* and *procedural* memories. *Semantic* and *episodic* memories are known jointly as declarative memory. Semantic memory refers to general knowledge independent from specific events, which is believed to be stored as a network of concepts. Episodic memory contains information about specific individual experiences, including time of event occurrence and context [13]. Procedural memory is a skill-based memory referring to the implicit knowledge of how to do things, which may be accessible only through performance [14].

Meaning structures define the ways we organize data to make sense of them [15]. Developing meaning structures is to identify relations in data, such as categorization, part–whole relations, cause–effect relations, sequence relations, and so on. The meaning structure of individuals can be classified as *private, accessible,* and *collective*. The private meaning structure is composed of organizational members' cognitive maps, which they choose to withhold from other members. The accessible meaning structure is built by an individual's cognitive map, which he/she is willing to make available to others. The collective meaning structure is the cognitive maps, which organizational members hold jointly with other members.

We view individual memory as a system composed of internal and external components by generalizing various individual memory theories as shown in Figure 2a. The internal component is composed of two layers: the upper layer containing declarative and procedural knowledge, and the lower layer containing private and accessible meaning structures. External component denotes an interface to gain knowledge from various knowledge sources.

The collective mind is not only viewed as a composite of individual minds, but also referred to the social process of articulating, exchanging, and sharing informa-

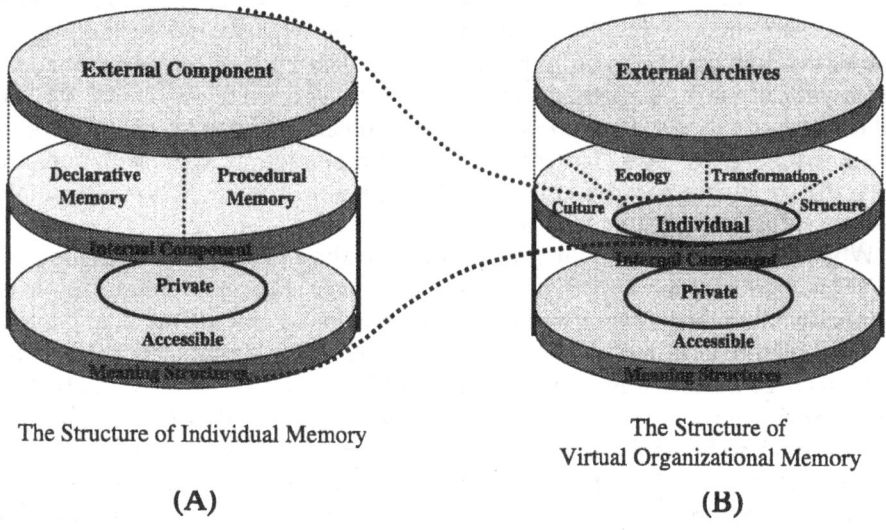

Figure 2. The structure of individual and virtual organizational memories.

tion in leading to common interpretations [16]. Organizational memory is an instance of collective memory, which relies on knowledge spatially distributed throughout the processes, individuals, and artifacts of the organization and beyond its boundaries [14]. Organizational memory is vital for the effectiveness and learning of an organization [17].

The four ontological levels of knowledge (individual, group, organization, and interorganization) differentiate the various memory and meaning structures. Entities within these four ontological levels should keep their own memory and retain the interaction between entities at the same level to higher ontological levels. Organizational memory can be viewed as the composition of six bins: *individuals, culture, transformations, structures, ecology,* and *external archives* [18]. Organizational memory must include direct experiences and observations of individuals in a suitable format that matches individual cognitive orientations and value systems. Organizational culture is a learned way of perceiving, thinking, and feeling about problems that are transmitted by members of the organization to the organization. Transformations are business processes occurring within an organization. Organizational structure must be considered in light of its implications for individual roles and its link with the environment. Individual roles provide a repository in which organizational information can be stored. The actual physical structure or workplace ecology of an organization encodes and thus, reveals a great deal of information about the organization. External archives help recall particular events when an individual's memory fails.

Organizational memory can be viewed as a static storage, and dynamic operations are needed to activate it. Stein and Zwass [14] identified these operations as mnemonic functions, and separated them into *acquisition, retention, maintenance, search,* and *retrieval,* to describe manipulation of the organizational memory. Acquisition gathers the data, information, and knowledge from all available sources.

Retention is the location that composes the structure of memory. Memories are maintained to make accessible by deciding how and when to update or delete files. The search function seeks more information, which updates, corrects, or adds to the organizational base. Retrieval is the process that organizational memory can be called forth to support decision making and problem solving [14, 18–20]. From the aforementioned reviews, we realize the static storage as representations, and meaning structures and dynamic operations as mnemonic functions to maintain the individual and organizational memories.

What should compose a virtual organizational memory? Because members of a VO are generally spatially distributed, have fewer chances to communicate face to face, mostly rely on expertise of various domains to execute tasks, and interact in a less hierarchical organization, the individual bin is designated as the core of a virtual organizational memory acting as a hub linking other bins. In Figure 2b, we portray a virtual organizational memory structured by internal component and external archives. Based on Walsh and Ungson's [18] six bins of organizational memory, we place the individual bin to the core of the upper layer of the internal component, and the individual bin is surrounded by the other four bins: culture, ecology, transformation, and structure. The individual bin depicted in Figure 2a is centered to represent a large pool of individual memories within the VO. In the lower layer of the internal component, the private meaning structure is akin to individual memory to represent the portion of knowledge the VO withholds from other organizations. The accessible meaning structure specifies the knowledge shared with other organizations. The external archives link to relevant sources such as other members of participant organizations, who do not belong to the VO.

The concept of transactive memory can fit in our description about virtual organizational memory and may shed light on VOL. Transactive memory describes how people in close relationships share cognition, which means a shared system for encoding, storing, and retrieving information. Transactive memory systems have two major components: (a) the individual memories of the members and (b) the transactive processes that construct and use these individual memories to provide the group access to a larger pool of collective knowledge [21]. For example, a husband may not know where to find candles around the house, for instance, but may still be able to find them in a blackout by asking his wife to describe the location. The transactive process starts when individuals learn something about each other's domains of expertise, and thus, enables the group to perform as in an efficient memory system. A directory of expertise plays an important role in achieving efficient memory access capacity. A directory-sharing computer network can be used as a model for describing a transactive memory system [22]. It consists of three key processes: (a) *directory updating*, whereby people learn what others are likely to know; (b) *information allocation*, by which new information is communicated to the person whose expertise will facilitate its storage; and (c) *retrieval coordination*, which is a plan for retrieving needed information on any topics based on related knowledge from individual expertise in the memory system. In Section 4, we further describe how the concept of transactive memory contributes to our VOL model.

3. ORGANIZATIONAL LEARNING

Among organizational learning theories and models proposed in recent years, Huber's [23] four constructs have been widely accepted. These four constructs are (a) *knowledge acquisition*, the process by which knowledge is obtained; (b) *information distribution*, the process by which information from different sources is shared and thereby leads to new information or understanding; (c) *information interpretation*, the process by which distributed information is given one or more commonly understood interpretations; and (d) *organizational memory*, the means by which knowledge is stored for future use.

An organization is composed of individuals, and an organization ultimately learns via its individual members [24]. Individual learning is a process where knowledge is created through the transformation of experience, and the learning progress is an experiential learning cycle [25]. Learning may occur under at least two conditions [10]. First, learning occurs when an organization achieves what it intended; that is, there is a match between its design for action and the actuality or outcome. Second, learning occurs when a mismatch between intentions and outcomes is identified and it is corrected; that is, a mismatch is turned into a match. *Single-loop learning* occurs when mismatches are created and then corrected by changing actions. *Double-loop learning* occurs when mismatches are corrected by altering the governing structure and, in turn, the behaviors as well. The governing structure is the preferred theory an individual applies to solve problems. To achieve effective organizational learning process, an organization does not only simply encourage its members to exchange their accessible meaning structures with each other; but also must actively facilitate collective learning in a cycle of *generating, integrating, interpreting*, and *acting* on information [26]. It consists of four steps: (a) widespread generation of information, (b) integration of new or local information into the organization context, (c) collective interpretation of information, and (d) having authority to take responsible actions based on the interpreted meaning.

The transfer mechanism between individual and organization is the heart of organizational learning [23]. Among theories surveyed and listed in Table 1, the SECI model of knowledge creation proposed by Nonaka [27] is relatively comprehensive in both ontology and epistemology dimensions. The SECI model treats the knowledge transference between individual and organization as a spiral learning process interflowing with tacit and explicit knowledge. The SECI model contains four knowledge conversion processes:

1. *Socialization* enables the sharing of tacit knowledge between individuals and emphasizes that tacit knowledge is exchanged through joint activities, such as apprentices work with their mentors and learn craftsmanship not through language but by observation, imitation, and practice.
2. *Externalization* requires the expression of tacit knowledge and its translation into comprehensible forms that can be understood by others. Self-transcendence is a key to group integration and the conversion of tacit knowledge to explicit knowledge.
3. *Combination* creates new explicit knowledge from explicit knowledge through social processes to combine different bodies of explicit knowledge held by

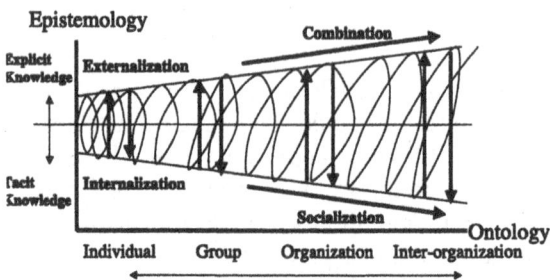

Figure 3. The spiral model of organizational knowledge creation [26].

individuals. The key issues are mainly in the communication, diffusion, and systemization of knowledge transcending the group.

4. *Internalization* converts explicit knowledge to tacit knowledge and embodies the explicit knowledge by using simulations or experiments to trigger the learning-by-doing process.

Figure 3 illustrates the spiral learning process and knowledge creation from individual, group, organization, to interorganizational level. The tacit knowledge embedded with individuals is the basis of organizational knowledge transfer and creation. Through externalization, an individual tacit knowledge can be conceptualized as explicit knowledge. In combining explicit knowledge across individual and organizational boundaries, knowledge can be synthesized into more systematic and executable instructions. While executing the instructions, individuals in the business processes internalize these coded instructions as tacit skills, which are possessed by individuals. The knowledge conversion cycle strengthens the problem-solving capability of the organizations and, in turn, renders a paradigm of learning organizations. The SECI model can help us to understand the virtue of VOL because a VO can be composed of a junction of individuals, groups, and organizations. Also, the dichotomy of tacit and explicit knowledge may help us to understand the role of each building block of the proposed VOL model in the next section.

4. VOL MODEL

4.1 Learning in a VO

Learning in a VO can be distinguished from traditional organizational learning or other interorganizational learning (e.g., strategic alliance, joint venture) by two characteristics: *IT orientation* and *social network augmentation*. IT orientation facilitates the capture and transfer of explicit knowledge. In this perspective, a knowledge map is applicable to contribute to VOL. The concept of a knowledge map is derived from influence diagrams capturing the diverse information possessed by an individual or a group [28]. A knowledge map is the visual display of captured information and relationships, which enables the communication and learning of knowledge by observers with different backgrounds at multiple levels of detail [29, 30]. The individual items of intellectual capital included in such a map can be text, sound, graphics, models, or numbers. Maps can also serve as links to implicit knowledge sources, such as experts. An effective knowledge map must evolve through actions and remain up to date. They must also be able to exploit this intellectual capital by making this knowledge accessible to everyone at every level of the organization in appropriate forms of display [29].

A social network can be viewed as a set of nodes (e.g., persons, organizations) linked by a set of social relationships (e.g., friendships, transfer of funds, overlapping membership) [31]. The social network can be viewed as the individual bin combining with external archives to facilitate the sourcing of knowledge. A VO has shorter longevity collaborating with participants compared with strategic alliances, but not as short as one-shot contact to diminish the chance of germinating the trust. In this perspective, social network augmentation enlarges the span of knowledge sources to enhance the learning in VO [32].

To facilitate learning in VOs, questions often asked are how to integrate partial knowledge of individuals from different organizations and enhance the sparks of interaction between members when face-to-face communication is unavailable. We face the problem of gathering and coordinating these fragments to form a coherent and complete knowledge to solve problems in a VO. Demsetz [26] identified direction as the principal means by which knowledge can be communicated at low cost between specialists and the large number of other persons who are either specialists or nonspecialists in other domains. In summary, knowledge maps may serve as directories pointing to articulated memory items, and social networks serve as directories pointing to individuals withholding the needed but inarticulate memory items. Therefore, the transactive memory concept described in Section 2 may help elaborate learning in a VO.

4.2 VOL Model

In this subsection, we propose a VOL model to formally elaborate learning in a VO. By proposing the VOL model, we hope to fill the vacancy of learning and memory in VOs denoted in Table 1. We view a VOL model as a transactive memory system. A transactive memory system is defined as follows:

$T_{mem} = \langle K_{map}, S_{net}, M_{fun} \rangle$, where T_{mem} denotes transactive memory,
$K_{map} = \langle K_{obj}, K_{dep} \rangle$ denotes knowledge map represented by knowledge objects (K_{obj}) and the dependency between knowledge objects (K_{dep}),
$S_{net} = \langle I, R, S_{link} \rangle$ denotes social network formed with individuals (I), their relationship (R), and the strength of the relationship (S_{link}), and
$M_{fun} = \langle K_{allocate}, S_{update}, K_{maintain}, R_{collaborate} \rangle$ represents mnemonic functions including knowledge allocation ($K_{allocate}$), social network updating (S_{update}), knowledge maintenance ($K_{maintain}$), and collaborative knowledge retrieval ($R_{collaborate}$).

Figure 4 illustrates the proposed VOL model. Individuals with individual memory systems from different organizations form a VO in which individual memory contains declarative and procedural knowledge by the meaning structure in various private and accessible degrees. Through external components of an individual memory system, which connects together as a social network, we hope to generate the collective meaning structure by linking complementary core competencies of participants.

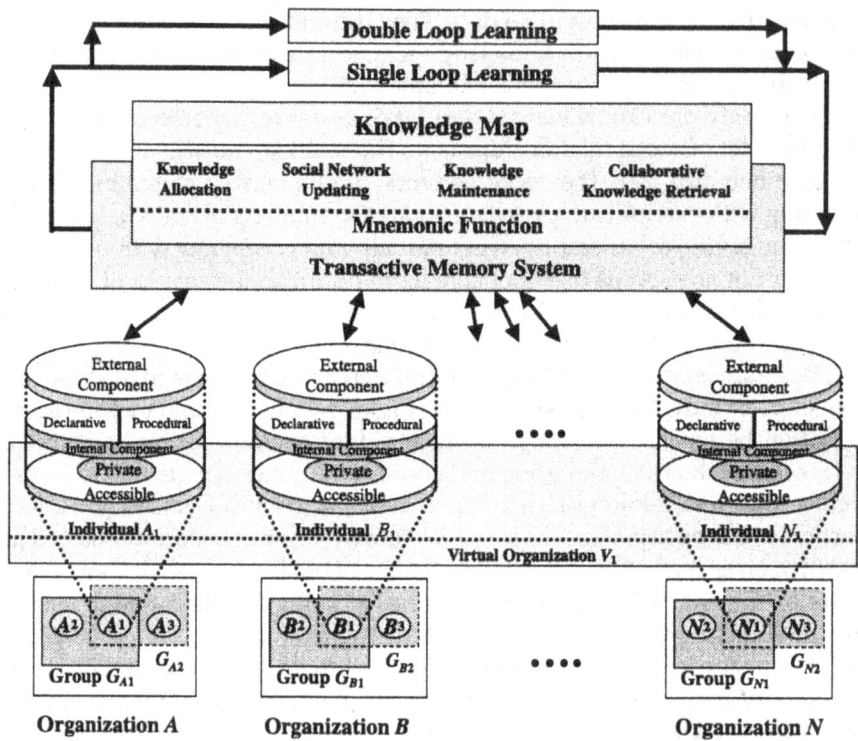

Figure 4. A virtual organizational learning model.

In the VOL model, a knowledge map captures the knowledge covered in a VO. It is represented by ontology in context (e.g., enterprise ontology) and content (e.g., domain ontology) to link knowledge type and their dependencies in certain business processes. We propose four main mnemonic functions, which compose the knowledge mapping system, to manage knowledge map in a VO.

1. *Knowledge allocation function:* links knowledge objects of knowledge maps to individuals of social networks, so that specific knowledge can be allocated through social networks. Agent-based technologies [e.g., 33] and skills-based management [34] can be applied here.

2. *Social network updating function:* refreshes the relationship between individuals during the interaction along the evolution of a VO. Technologies such as data mining in conjunction with skills-based management concepts [34], attributed relational graphs [35], and multiagent systems (e.g., Socialware) [36] are suitable for the task.

3. *Knowledge maintenance function:* maintains the knowledge map from performing business processes in a VO by inserting, modifying, or deleting knowledge objects and their dependencies. Bayesian networks (e.g., [37]), automatic thesaurus generation for ontology construction (e.g., [38]), and document analysis techniques such as PAT–Tree (e.g., [39]) mutual information calculation (e.g., [40]),

term-weighting system [41], document similarity [42, 43], and hierarchical clustering [44] are applicable.

4. *Collaborative knowledge retrieval function:* retrieves problem-solving or decision-making related knowledge by collaboratively accessing the transactive memory of individuals. Search engines, role-based access control (e.g., [45]), and intelligent information retrieval algorithms are related technologies.

The learning scenario in the VOL model can be elaborated according to the SECI model as follows: Individuals within a VO may initially perform their tasks by utilizing their existing expertise stored in individual memory or their organizational memory systems. They may have fewer chances to communicate face to face due to the virtual setting, and hence hinder the socialization process from occurring. The social network updating function may help individuals to identify champions or experts in specific domains and link them with certain relationships, such as sharing similar interests or accessing the same knowledge objects. The bridges between participants may increase the chance of socialization processes to take place. When they try to articulate their knowledge and make it accessible for others, no matter whether voluntarily or pushed by a certain incentive system, they are undergoing the externalization process. Because a VO is usually formed by organizations with complementary core competencies, it is common that individuals need to coordinate and collaborate in performing joint business processes. The knowledge allocation function captures and organizes codified knowledge from knowledge contributors to the knowledge map. The social network updating function stimulates experts to articulate their knowledge and then to shrink their private meaning structure to share with knowledge requesters. If these experts fail to provide requested knowledge, they may search for other possible sources or employ their own social networks to link to possible knowledge providers beyond the VO to retrieve the requested knowledge. Therefore, knowledge providers may learn something during the knowledge searching process and then codify the knowledge to return to the knowledge requesters. The new codified knowledge will also be captured into the knowledge map. Sometimes the knowledge maps also serve as languages to help individuals learn unfamiliar domain knowledge and smooth the communication process. In the combination process, the knowledge allocation function is essential to integrate relevant knowledge, and the knowledge maintenance function keeps the knowledge map up to date. The collaborative knowledge retrieval function acquires decision alternatives in facilitating the problem-solving process in a VO through knowledge map and social network. Finally, people actually learn when knowledge is internalized. They may detect conflicting requirements and try to resolve those conflicts by changing prevailing norms, values, and systems during the interaction with the transactive memory system, and thus, the learning process is promoted from single-loop learning into double-loop learning. The continued augmenting process of learning is expressed as single- and double-loop learning in the VOL model in Figure 4.

The transactive memory system is an important mechanism to accelerate learning in VOs. The merits of the transactive memory system are identified as follows:

1. Knowledge map can be created quickly and maintained easier in a VO. As a temporary and quickly formed network, members in VOs may encounter several situations to take part in a totally new-formed group. Rulke and Rau [45] found that newly formed groups spent time discussing their expertise. Hollingshead [46] also learned from a laboratory experiment that when communication is allowed, strangers begin to develop a transactive memory system by explicitly establishing relative expertise when working on a knowledge-pooling task. A knowledge map can be created quickly and maintained easier in VOs, in which business processes mostly operate on IT-supported platforms, and explicit knowledge is more easily captured into the knowledge map.

2. Relative expertise of members in a VO can be easily identified. Members with different expertise may be spatially distributed in organizations. Also, each person needs an accurate representation to know who to ask for needed information [47, 48]. Social networks work as a directory to the relative expertise of members in VOs, and thus, enable members to know who knows what and where to find the right person to ask. The social network updating function refreshes the continuously evolving organizational memory and enables employees to learn through navigating the network as well as through the discovery of new relationships [29].

3. Facilitate faster job training and role orientation for individuals in a VO. When new individuals or reassigned employees come in, they have no connections to the virtual organizational memory. With a transactive memory system, workers can orient themselves by identifying their organizational roles, specifying their assigned responsibilities, and the available support resources [29]. It also prevents the fragmented learning proposed by Kim [24] from taking place in VOs.

4. Provide integrated and relevant knowledge to members in a VO. An individual's ability to integrate knowledge is constrained by cognitive limits, and it is not feasible for each individual to try to learn all knowledge possessed by other specialists [48]. With the help of the collaborative knowledge retrieval function of a transactive memory system, knowledge falling into the same category can be integrated, and relevant knowledge about events of interest can be also accessed.

5. Make mental model explicit and allow people with expertise in many different domains in a VO to communicate with each other. Knowledge map is a tool or language to make the shared mental model explicit, it permits gradual collection of knowledge in an increasing quantitative form, and thus allows people with expertise in many different domains to communicate with each other and to contribute their knowledge to solving problems [30]. As mental models are made explicit and actively shared, the base of shared meaning in an organization expands, the organization's capacity for effective coordinated action increases, and it may also accelerate individual learning [24].

6. Encourage people to share knowledge with others. Because the relationships in a social network are identified explicitly and people are upheld as experts in specific domains, they may feel responsible for providing requested knowledge to solve problems, and sometimes may contribute to the shrink of their private meaning structures and augment their accessible meaning structures. These effects are identified in Constant et al. [5] and Jarvenpaa et al. [6] to express the influences of prosocial attributes and organizational norms for experts to share knowledge.

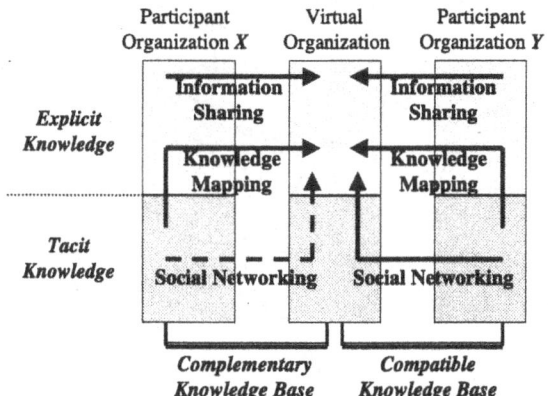

Figure 5. Knowledge transference in virtual organizational learning.

People may also feel free to ask stupid questions because asking for someone's help is what the social network subsystem inspires individuals to do.

Considering that participant organizations in a VO may have complementary and compatible knowledge bases, we can further dichotomize the learning in a VO into three approaches: *information sharing, knowledge mapping,* and *social networking* (shown in Figure 5). The knowledge transfer between two participant organizations utilizes the mnemonic functions of the VOL model. This viewpoint is based on the transfer of tacit and explicit knowledge between organizations, elaborated by Nonaka [50], to utilize organizational knowledge. With the information sharing approach, knowledge transfer is enabled through sharing information when both parties codify their knowledge into information. With the knowledge mapping approach, the transference of tacit knowledge of participating firms is facilitated by the knowledge mapping system described in the VOL model to convert tacit knowledge to explicit knowledge. With the social networking approach, the transference of tacit knowledge is triggered by socialization proposed by Nonaka [27], perhaps through the connection between individuals to transfer knowledge. However, participants with complementary knowledge due to lack of absorptive capacity (identified by [8]) may encounter a higher hurdle to learning drawn by the dashed line in Figure 5. We think the higher the trust between participant organizations, the more private meaning structures can be transformed into accessible meaning structures by these three approaches. Besides, different industries may prefer different learning approaches. For industries mostly facing structured problems, such as the provision of mature or standard products, they may heavily depend on the knowledge mapping and information sharing approaches than social networking because the captured knowledge is reusable. For industries mainly resolving unstructured problems, articulating the involved knowledge may be a tough or costly task, so that the social networking approach can deliver significant benefits.

In summary, most people encounter problems and resolve them by themselves or ask convenient people for help. People being asked are not always pro-

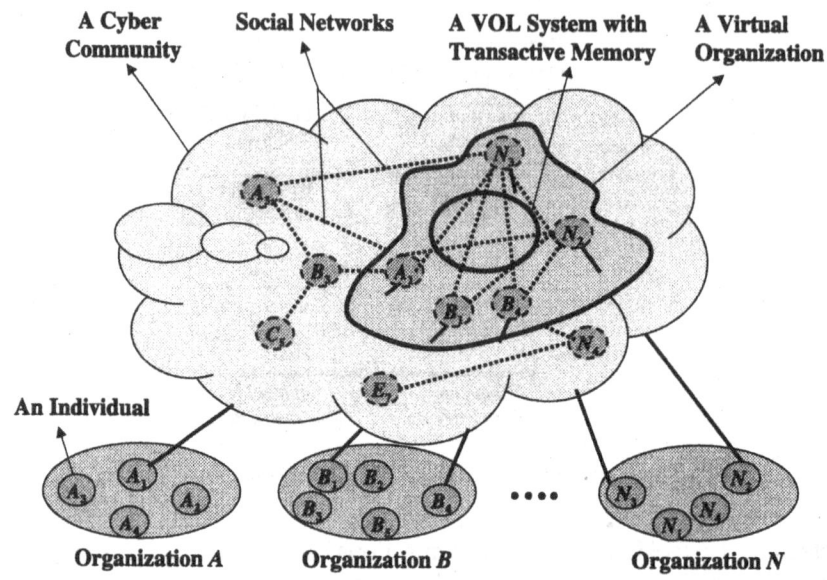

Figure 6. The transactive memory system in a cyber community.

fessionals, and only a small set of persons with limited backgrounds are involved, and the individual learning cycle is not connected with the organizational learning cycle whether in a physical or virtual setting. With a transactive memory system, domain experts from various real organizations with complementary and compatible knowledge bases are reachable to contribute their knowledge to combine with others. Also, the individual learning cycle linked with the organizational learning cycle is accelerated and strengthened by interacting with the knowledge map and social network through four mnemonic functions. In particular, when the VO is terminated, the knowledge maps and social networks are well preserved and serve as a profound foundation for the formation and operation of another VO.

5. VOL MODEL IN CYBER COMMUNITIES

As mentioned in Subsection 4.1 that VOL is more IT orientation and social network augmentation. We view a cyber community as a great foundation for forming VOs. The VOL model proposed in this article can be developed as a transactive memory system in cyber communities to facilitate the learning process.

Figure 6 illustrates how a transactive memory system exists in a cyber community, in which individuals come from physical organizations. Through social networks growing in the cyber community, individuals get to know each other in the virtual space, and of course, individual's mutual acquaintances may be enhanced or withheld by the physical connections. According to the four stages of life cycle of a VO as shown in Figure 1, the social networks embedded in a cyber community may facilitate the identification and formation of a VO. During the operation stage of a VO, the transactive memory system facilitates the learning cycle in the virtual space to improve the performance of business processes. The termination of a VO signifies the forgetting of the transactive memory due to the cessation of memory refresh and recall.

5.1 A Case: SCTNet

We have been developing a cyber community called the Smart Creative Teachers Network (SCTNet; http://sctnet.edu.tw) dedicated to supporting teachers at primary and junior high schools in Taiwan to share and create domain knowledge across organizational boundaries and develop VOs gradually (a snapshot of its opening Web page is shown in Figure 7). SCTNet reveals the purpose of establishing the professional learning community for boosting teachers' professional awareness and creativity in their educational practices. In Taiwan's educational reform, there is experimentation in small-class teaching with integrated curriculums, and teachers are struggling to find effective approaches to start this new educational practice. However, within their individual schools, the interaction of primary and junior high school teachers may be limited to their familiar colleagues, which may not be effective and efficient to launch the new educational practice.

A school is a professional organization staffed by teachers to perform teaching, research, and services; teachers from different schools can form VOs to perform common tasks and achieve better practice in their profession. Therefore, the SCTNet embedded with the transactive memory system can facilitate the identifi-

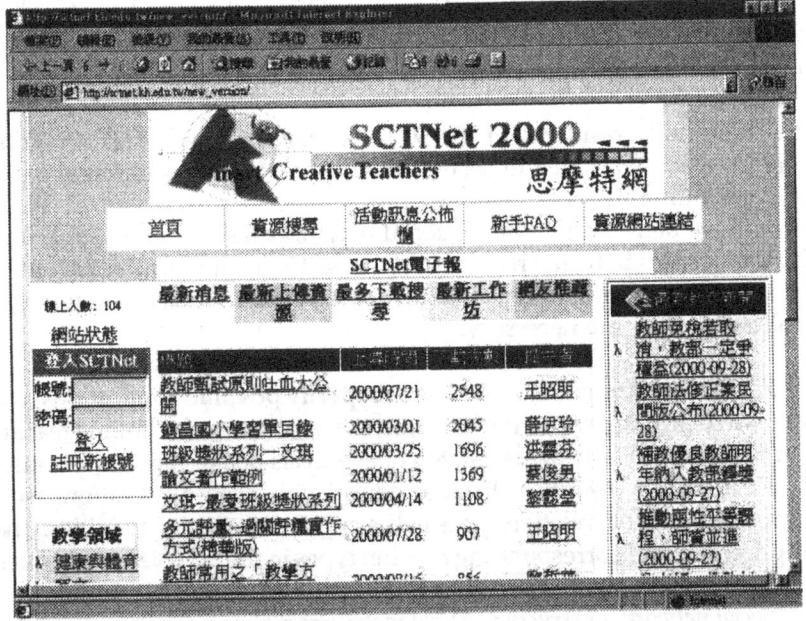

Figure 7. A snapshot of the Smart Creative Teachers Network (http://sctnet.edu.tw).

cation, formation, and operations of VOs for the teacher community in cyberspace. We are aiming at forming professional VOs to strengthen professionalism and then trigger the learning cycle when teachers interact with the transactive memory system. Moreover, teachers may share teaching materials and professional expertise through computer networks across school boundaries.

To facilitate learning across the organizational boundaries, we build the transactive memory system with a knowledge map and a social network in the SCTNet, in addition to the basic features of a cyber community for communications. Note that Chinese is a complex character-based language, and the involved techniques listed later may be modified when applied to other languages. First, we design the knowledge map as a visual display of domain knowledge category. The following steps illustrate the knowledge categorization for building a knowledge map:

1. *Text indexing:* Codified knowledge objects in Chinese text are indexed using the PAT–Tree indexing algorithm to increase processing efficiency of the following steps.
2. *Keyphrase (or keyword) extraction:* This employs statistical algorithms such as mutual information calculation to determine lexical patterns in terms of key phrases or keywords.
3. *Representative keyphrase (or keyword) determination:* This determines the representative key phrases (or keywords) for each document using term-weighting system techniques.
4. *Document clustering:* Documents with similar keywords can be clustered as a concept or a category of knowledge using various clustering techniques.
5. *Knowledge map visualization:* The derived hierarchical and clustered relations of concepts and documents are viewed graphically to guide the navigation in each domain.

The community residents of the SCTNet may perceive various merits of the knowledge map mentioned in Section 4, while interacting with other residents in this cyber community.

Second, we build and maintain social networks based on the explicit and implicit relationships between residents in the SCTNet community. We employ link analysis based on graph theory to discover interaction patterns between members. The following steps are necessary:

1. *Application identification:* We need to specify possible applications to support members in reaching people. For example, the application for linking teachers with similar teaching subjects to ask related questions is one of many applications.
2. *Relation type definition:* In accordance with each application, we should clearly define possible relation types in the cyber community activities. The possible applications and corresponding relation types in the SCTNet are enumerated in Table 2.
3. *Social network construction:* The construction of social networks includes the following steps: First, utilize the attributed relational graph to represent each relation type. Second, convert the attribute relational graph in the form of adjacency

Table 2
Social Network Functions Provided by the Smart Creative Teachers Network

Applications	Relationship Types
Allocating members with similar interests	Similar interested domains, uploading similar documents, downloading similar documents, similar discussion topics, and/or similar expertise
Searching for experts in a specific domain	Uploading significant amount of documents in a specific domain, and/or posting significant amount of articles in a specific domain
Seeking answers for specific topics from domain experts	Uploading significant amount of documents about the specific topics, and/or posting significant amount of articles about the specific topics
Searching for possible candidates to form a group	Similar interested domains, uploading similar documents, downloading similar documents, similar discussion topics, and/or similar expertise
Finding the champions in a special interest group	Posting significant amount of articles in the special interest group

matrix. Third, link members through matrix traversal operations. Finally, visualize the captured relationships between members.

4. *Social network maintenance:* The structure of captured relations can be influenced by relatively stable or dynamic activities between members. Personal interests may be relatively stable, but the publication status may be updated frequently. Therefore, the maintenance of social networks can be scheduled at different time scales. Currently, we update the social networks through periodical reconstruction, and incremental evolution can be tested in the future. With the implicit social network clearly constructed, more individualized services can be provided to facilitate interaction processes.

5.2 VOL in the SCTNet Cyber Community

In the users' view, SCTNet exhibits the following features:

1. Sharing domain knowledge and practical experiences between teachers from different schools across widespread regions: SCTNet provides a platform for teachers to upload curriculum designs, research results, and teaching experiences in various teaching domains. Other teachers as SCTNet members can download these publications and recommend with different degrees of confidence to other members. The teaching domains on the SCTNet include languages, mathematics, science and technology, sociology, arts and humanity, and physical education, and may include more domains along the growth of the community. SCTNet members can interact through discussion boards, online chat, and e-mail. In addition, a dedicated environment is also available for members to form special interest groups to collaborate for project execution.

2. Awarding teachers for publishing their professional expertise: Efforts are made to encourage knowledge sharing between members, such as contribution awards and domain expert titles. Uploaded materials recommended by the

SCTNet colleagues are delivered to members with similar domains proactively through the electronic newsletter, called *SCT Newsletter*.

3. Encouraging teachers to learn actively assisted by personal knowledge map: The SCTNet plays a role as a spontaneous learning assistant in such an active learning environment with the active recommendation system and the knowledge map navigation system. Assisted by the personal knowledge map, members may have a whole picture of specific teaching domain, and then have the strategies to bridge the gap of needed knowledge for being an effective teacher. This may help to increase learning efficiency and alleviate frustration in their professional development to some extent.

4. Enabling the construction of teacher professional social network: SCTNet as the platform of the teacher community enables teachers to access knowledge possessed by other teachers as the known or ambiguous relationships between members are delineated explicitly or implicitly. The construction of social networks can facilitate finding colleagues to collaborate for a range of purposes, such as solving common problems or forming virtual teams to execute specific projects.

5. Activating the learning cycles of the VO: The aforementioned functions include knowledge allocation, social network updating, knowledge map maintenance, and collaborative knowledge retrieval, which in turn activate the learning cycles of the VO for teachers.

To elaborate how school teachers learn and create knowledge along the life cycle of a VO in an SCTNet cyber community, we use a scenario of describing how school teachers collaborate with each other unrestricted by school boundaries to teach hyperactive pupils. The story starts from a math teacher, Susan, frustrated by a hyperactive student in her class. She posted her questions on the special education discussion board of the SCTNet. With the knowledge allocation function, Susan identified articles related to attention deficit and hyperactivity disorder (ADHD) contributed by other SCTNet's members. She realized that ADHD is a behavioral syndrome where hyperactivity and inattention causes social and learning difficulties. Hyperactive children need much soft, gentle, continual, close, and intimate physical communications. ADHD children benefit from having complex physical toys and structures to manipulate. Games and toys that require several children to manipulate and to move are relaxing and improve the post school behavior of children. The more physical activity the ADHD child experiences, the calmer he/she becomes. Susan practiced what guidelines she obtained from SCTNet contributed by other teachers. Susan's colleague, Peter, had one student in his class with ADHD. Peter knew that the student was taking the medicine Ritalin™. Ritalin™, also known as methylphenidate, is used to treat people with ADHD, and is being prescribed to help students stay awake during intense last-minute cramming sessions. Susan and Peter interacted about ADHD cases to practice feasible class management strategies to help hyperactive students. This socialization process enabled them to exchange their experiences in person. After a semester's practice, Susan and Peter published their experiences in caring for ADHD pupils to the SCTNet, which is an externalization process. This article was assigned to a Health and Physical Education category according to the knowledge maintenance function and then recommended to other similar interest teachers registered in the SCTNet community. Another teacher, Mary, responded to Susan and Peter's article. Mary had been a counseling teacher working with ADHD cases for several years, and after analyzing Susan and Peter's cases, she suggested cautious use of Ritalin™, which may cause brain damage for developing children. Other comments from a doctor described the side effects of overusing Ritalin™. By combining the knowledge contributed by experts from other organizations, Susan and Peter revised their attitudes and actions in teaching hyperactive students, which is the internalization process in Nonaka's [27] SECI model.

The knowledge of teaching ADHD students in a SCTNet community is stored, maintained, and retrieved through the knowledge map and social network of the transactive memory system. A group of teachers who are teaching or have been teaching ADHD students can form a special interest group (SIG) focusing on sharing experiences in teaching ADHD students and, in turn, creating new practices in caring for ADHD pupils. The collaborative knowledge retrieval function facilitates the efficient allocation of problem-solving strategies. As education reform moves toward small-class teaching with integrated curriculum, teachers are eager to pay more attention to students' differences and help them more effectively. Susan and Peter established an ADHD Children Education Association (ACEA) in SCTNet. It is a VO dedicated to help teachers and parents to take care of hyperactive children. Through the acquaintance of community residents with the help of social network functions, the ACEA was established in a very efficient way in identifying potential schools and teachers and forming the organization. The operation of ACEA is based on SCTNet's SIG to coordinate core management team members and to accumulate organizational memory of governing practice. The cyber community on the SCTNet is the target market and potential partner. Such VO may be terminated as the goals are accomplished or the mission canceled. The transactive memory system retains the knowledge map and social network after the termination of the VO.

Through the aforementioned scenario, we demonstrate the transactive memory system embedded in the SCTNet for the teacher professional community. The SECI cycle across organizations and the life cycle of a VO are illustrated to realize the VOL model. The SCTNet is a cyber professional community for teachers specializing in primary and junior high school education. It is also a VOL platform for professional teachers in various subject domains to join together from many physical organizations, and it is aimed at forming professional VOs to strengthen professionalism. By virtue of VOL capability on the SCTNet, the school becomes agile to adapt to new education, and teachers create new knowledge to strengthen their professional ability. By continuously improving user interfaces, interaction mechanisms, and embedded VOL capability, we anticipate that SCTNet can facilitate the growth of the professional social networks and establish the paradigm of VOL in the future.

6. CONCLUSIONS

We propose a conceptual model for VOL and describe the transactive memory system, especially in a cyber community. The transactive memory composed of social network, knowledge map, and mnemonic functions is a suitable mechanism for developing virtual organizational memory. Based on knowledge conversion across individual and organization, the transactive memory system can serve as the core technology in synthesizing tacit or explicit knowledge from organizations with complementary or compatible knowledge bases. A cyber community for teachers, SCTNet, has been developed in different schools across Taiwan to illustrate the VOL model. The transactive memory system with knowledge map and social network is embedded in SCTNet to activate the learning cycles of VOs and move toward the VOL paradigm.

Compared with learning in other interorganizational structures, such as strategic alliance and joint venture, the VOL model utilizes the merits of VOs in IT orientation and social network augmentation to facilitate learning across identification, formation, operation, and termination stages of a VO.

In future research, we will further develop the components and functions for a transactive memory system for specific business applications and other cyber communities. Through implementation, we can revise the VOL model to make it more effective for facilitating learning in VOs. Although such issues as trust and attitude toward information sharing in global virtual teams or within an organization have been investigated in the literature [5, 6], the learning behaviors of individuals and the role of trust in a VOs in terms of knowledge sharing and creation need to be further investigated. Some interventions may be applied to obtain findings regarding the learning effects under different organizational norms and individual learning styles. We plan to verify the SECI knowledge creation model, proposed by Nonaka [27], in educational organizations.

We aim to establish a paradigm in learning across organizations in three categories: (a) steering the group learning wheel, (b) pursuing double-loop learning, and (c) establishing virtual professional organizations. Our empirical study hopes to examine this paradigm shift and hopefully shed light on better learning and knowledge creation in virtual communities. The formulation of knowledge-sharing culture, concerns of privacy and security in social network construction, and the role of interorganizational memory are also interesting issues for further studies.

REFERENCES

[1] S. L. Goldman, R. N. Nagel, and K. Preiss, *Agile Competitors and Virtual Organizations: Strategies for Enriching the Customer.* New York: Van Nostrand Reinhold, 1995.

[2] T. J. Strader, F. R. Lin, and M. J. Shaw, "Information infrastructure for electronic virtual organization management," *Decision Support Systems*, vol. 23, no. 1, pp. 75–94, 1998.

[3] F.-R. Lin and M. J. Shaw, "Reengineering the order fulfillment process in supply chain networks," *International Journal of Flexible Manufacturing Systems*, vol. 10, no. 3, pp. 197–229, 1998.

[4] D. Bottoms, "Back to the future," *Industry Week*, vol. 243, no. 18, pp. 61–64, 1994.

[5] D. Constant, S. Kiesler, and L. Sproull, "What's mine is ours, or is it? A study of attitudes about information sharing," *Information Systems Research*, vol. 5, no. 4, pp. 400–421, 1994.

[6] S. L. Jarvenpaa, K. Knoll, and D. E. Leidner, "Is anybody out there? Antecedents of trust in global virtual teams," *Journal of Management Information Systems*, vol. 14, no. 4, pp. 29–64, 1998.

[7] O. Shenkar and J. Li, "Knowledge search in international cooperative ventures," *Organization Science*, vol. 10, no. 2, pp. 134–143, 1999.

[8] W. Cohen and D. Levinthal, "Absorptive capacity: A new perspective on learning and innovation," *Administrative Science Quarterly*, vol. 35, no. 1, pp. 128–152, 1990.

[9] S. Balakrishnan and M. P. Koza, "Information asymmetry, adverse selection and joint ventures," *Journal of Economic Behavior and Organization*, vol. 20, pp. 99–117, 1993.

[10] C. Argyris and D. Schon, *Organizational Learning: A Theory of Action Perspective*. Reading, MA: Addison-Wesley, 1978.
[11] H. W. Chesbrough and D. J. Teece, "When is virtual virtuous? Organizing for innovation," *Harvard Business Review*, vol. 74, no. 1, pp. 65–72, 1996.
[12] A. V. Steil, R. M. Barcia, and C. S. Pacheco, "An approach to learning in virtual organizations," *Electronic Journal of Organizational Virtualness*, vol. 1, no. 1, pp. 69–88, 1999.
[13] E. Tulving, *Elements of Episodic Memory*. Oxford, England: Oxford University Press, 1983.
[14] E. W. Stein and V. Zwass, "Actualizing organizational memory with information systems," *Information Systems Research*, vol. 6, no. 2, pp. 85–117, 1995.
[15] N. M. Dixon, *The Organizational Learning Cycle: How We Can Learn Collectively*. New York: McGraw-Hill, 1994.
[16] M. Halbwachs, *The Collective Memory* (F. J. Ditter and V. Y. Ditter, Eds. Translation of 1950 Original). New York: Harper Colophon, 1950/1980.
[17] R. Duncan and A. Weiss, "Organizational learning: Implications for organizational design," in *Research in Organizational Behavior*, B. Staw, Ed., vol. 1 Greenwich, CT: JAI, 1979, pp. 75–123.
[18] J. P. Walsh and G. R. Ungson, "Organizational memory," *Academy of Management Journal*, vol. 16, no. 1, pp. 57–91, 1991.
[19] G. Hackbarth and V. Grover, "The knowledge repository: Organizational memory information systems," *Information Systems Management*, vol. 16, no. 3, pp. 21–30, Summer 1999.
[20] K. Krippendorff, "Some principles of information storage and retrieval in society," *General Systems*, vol. 20, pp. 15–35, 1975.
[21] D. M. Wegner, "Transactive memory: A contemporary analysis of the group mind," in *Theories of Group Behavior*, B. Mullen and G. R. Goethals, Eds. New York: Springer-Verlag, 1986, pp. 185–208.
[22] D. M. Wegner, "A computer network model of human transactive memory," *Social Cognition*, vol. 13, no. 3, pp. 319–339, 1995.
[23] G. P. Huber, "Organizational learning: The contributing processes and the literatures," *Organization Science*, vol. 2, no. 1, pp. 88–117, 1991.
[24] D. H. Kim, "The link between individual and organizational learning," *Sloan Management Review*, vol. 35, no. 1, pp. 37–50, 1993.
[25] D. A. Kalb, *Experiential Learning*. Englewood Cliffs, NJ: Prentice-Hall, 1984.
[26] H. Demsetz, "The theory of the firm revisited," in *The Nature of the Firm*, O. E. Williamson and S. Winter, Eds. New York: Oxford University Press, 1991, pp. 159–178.
[27] I. Nonaka, "A dynamic theory of organizational knowledge creation," *Organization Science*, vol. 5, no. 1, pp. 14–37, 1994.
[28] R. A. Howard and J. E. Matheson, "Influence diagrams," in *Readings on the Principles and Applications of Decision Analysis*, R. A. Howard and J. E. Matheson, Eds., vol. 2. Menlo Park, CA: Strategic Decisions Group, 1984.
[29] F. V. Edmond III, "Knowledge mapping: Getting started with knowledge management," *Information Systems Management*, vol. 16, no. 4, pp. 16–23, Fall 1999.
[30] R. A. Howard, "Knowledge map," *Management Science*, vol. 35, no. 8, pp. 903–922, 1989.
[31] E. O. Lawman, J. Galaskiewicz, and P. V. Marston, "Community structure as inter-organizational linkages," *Annual Review of Sociology*, vol. 4, pp. 455–484, 1978.
[32] D. Meyerson, K. E. Wick, and R. M. Kramer, "Swift trust and temporary groups," in *Trust in Organizations: Frontiers of Theory and Research*, R. M. Kramer and T. R. Tyler, Eds. Thousand Oaks, CA: Sage, 1996, pp. 166–195.
[33] H. C. Tu and J. Hsiang, "An architecture and category knowledge for intelligent information retrieval agents," in *Proc. 31st Hawaii Int. Conf. on System Sciences (HCSS '98)*, IEEE, 1998, pp. 405–414.
[34] H. Riel, "Managing with skills," *Ives Business Journal*, vol. 62, no. 4, pp. 50–54, 1998.
[35] W.-H. Tsai and K.-S. Fu, "Error-correcting isomorphisms of attributed relational graphs for pattern analysis," *IEEE Transactions on Systems, Man, and Cybernetics*, vol. 9, no. 12, pp. 757–768, 1979.
[36] F. Hattor, T. Ohguro, M. Yokoo, S. Matsubara, and S. Yoshida, "Socialware: Multiagent systems for supporting network communities," *Comm. of the ACM*, vol. 42, no. 3, pp. 55–61, 1999.
[37] D. Heckerman and R. Shachter, "A Bayesian approach for learning causal networks," in *Uncertainty in Artificial Intelligence: Proc. Eleventh Conf.*, 1995, pp. 285–295.

[38] A. Abecker, A. Bernardi, K. Hinkelmann, O. Kuhn, and M. Sintek, "Toward a technology for organizational memories," *IEEE Intelligent Systems*, vol. 13, no. 3, pp. 40–48, 1998.
[39] T. H. Ong and H. Chen, "Updateable PAT-tree approach to Chinese key phrase extraction using mutual information: A linguistic foundation for knowledge management," in *Proc. 2nd Asian Digital Libraries Conf.*, 1999. Available on the World Wide Web: http://ross.lis.nut.edu.tw/ad199
[40] C. C. Yang, H. Ten, S. K. Yung, and A. K. L. Chung, "Chinese indexing using mutual information," *Proc. 1st Asia Digital Library Workshop*, 1998, pp. 57–64.
[41] G. Salton and C. Buckley, "A vector-space model for automatic indexing," *Comm. of the ACM*, vol. 18, no. 11, pp. 613–620, 1975.
[42] T. Biru, A. EL_Hamdouchi, R. S. Rees, and P. Willett, "Inclusion of relevance information in the term discrimination model," *The Journal of Documentation*, vol. 45, no. 2, pp. 85–100, 1989.
[43] G. Galton, "Generation and search of clustered files," *ACM Transaction on Database System*, vol. 3, no. 4, pp. 321–346, 1978.
[44] L. Kaufman and P. J. Rousseeuw, *Finding Group in Data: An Introduction to Cluster Analysis.* New York: Wiley, 1990.
[45] T. Hildmann and J. Bartholdt, "Managing trust between collaborating companies using outsourced role based access control," in *Proc. 4th ACM Workshop on Role-Based Access Control*, 1999, pp. 105–111.
[46] D. L. Rulke and D. Rau, "Investigating the encoding process of transactive memory development in group training," *Group Organization Management*, vol. 25, no. 4, pp. 373–396, 2000.
[47] A. B. Hollingshead, "Retrieval processes in transactive memory systems," *Journal of Personality and Social Psychology*, vol. 74, no. 3, pp. 659–671, 1998.
[48] D. M. Wegner, R. Erber, and P. Raymond, "Transactive memory in close relationships," *Journal of Personality and Social Psychology*, vol. 61, no. 6, pp. 923–929, 1991.
[49] R. M. Grant, "Prospering in dynamically-competitive environments: Organizational capability as knowledge integration," *Organization Science*, vol. 7, no. 4, pp. 375–387, 1996.
[50] I. Nonaka, P. Reinmoeller, and D. Senoo, "The 'ART' of knowledge: Systems to capitalize on market knowledge," *European Management Journal*, vol. 16, no. 6, pp. 673–684, 1998.
[51] D. A. Vollrath, B. H. Sheppard, V. B. Hinsz, and J. H. Davis, "Memory performance by decision-making groups and individuals," *Organizational Behavior and Human Decision Processes*, vol. 43, no. 3, pp. 289–300, 1989.
[52] R. Klimoski and S. Mohammed, "Team mental model: Construct or metaphor," *Journal of Management*, vol. 20, no. 2, pp. 403–437, 1994.
[53] A. P. Massey and W. A. Wallace, "Understanding and facilitating group problem structuring and formulation: Mental representations, interaction, and representation aids," *Decision Support Systems*, vol. 17, no. 4, pp. 253–274, 1996.
[54] J. W. Satzinger, "The creative process: The effects of group memory on individual idea generation," *Journal of Management Information Systems*, vol. 15, no. 4, pp. 143–160, 1999.
[55] J. J. Johnson, "An exploration of empowerment and organizational memory," *Journal of Managerial Issues*, vol. 10, no. 4, pp. 503–519, 1998.
[56] C. Moorman, "Organizational improvisation and organizational memory," *Academy of Management, The Academy of Management Review*, vol. 23, no. 4, pp. 698–723, 1998.
[57] G. Roth, "Developing organizational memory through learning histories," *Organizational Dynamics*, vol. 27, no. 2, pp. 43–60, 1998.
[58] E. W. Stein, "Organization memory: Review of concepts and recommendations for management," *International Journal of Information Management*, vol. 15, no. 1, pp. 17–32, 1995.
[59] F. Wijnhoven, "Designing organizational memories: Concept and method," *Journal of Organizational Computing and Electronic Commerce*, vol. 8, no. 1, pp. 29–55, 1998.
[60] M. D. Cohen "Individual learning and organizational routine," *Organization Science*, vol. 2, no. 1, pp. 135–139, 1991.
[61] D. M. Ezey, K. Ayas, and I. Gilad, "A dual-phase model for the individual learning process in individual tasks," *IIE Transactions*, vol. 27, no. 3, pp. 265–271, 1995.
[62] M. Martinez, "Using learning orientation to investigate how individuals learn successfully on the web," *Technical Communication*, vol. 46, no. 4, pp. 470–488, 1999.
[63] A. Mumford, "Individual and organizational learning—The pursuit of change," *Management Decision*, vol. 30, no. 6, pp. 143–148, 1992.

[64] J. Cohen, J. Ruffin, and L. Hillman, "Training and education in group relations: Some characteristics of the learning environment," *Human Relations*, vol. 34, no. 9, pp. 731–741, 1981.
[65] J. M. Donohue and J. B. Fox, "An investigation into the people-sequential heuristic method," *Decision Sciences*, vol. 24, no. 2, pp. 493–508, 1993.
[66] J. Harmon and J. Rohrbaugh, "Social judgment analysis and small group decision making: Cognitive feedback effects on individual and collective performance," *Organizational Behavior and Human Decision Processes*, vol. 46, no. 1, pp. 34–54, 1990.
[67] K. H. Lim, "An empirical study of computer system learning: Comparison of co-discovery and self-discovery methods," *Information Systems Research*, vol. 8, no. 3, pp. 254–272, 1997.
[68] V. McInerney, "Effects of metacognitive strategy training within a cooperative group learning context on computer achievement and anxiety: An aptitude-treatment interaction study," *Journal of Educational Psychology*, vol. 89, no. 4, pp. 686–695, 1997.
[69] M. Dodgson, "Organizational learning: A review of some literatures," *Organization Studies*, vol. 14, no. 3, pp. 375–394, 1993.
[70] S. M. Easterby, "Disciplines of organizational learning: Contributions and critiques," *Human Relations*, vol. 50, no. 9, pp. 1085–1113, 1997.
[71] C. M. Fiol and M. A. Lyles, "Organizational learning," *Academy of Management. The Academy of Management Review*, vol. 10, no. 4, pp. 803–813, 1985.
[72] B. Levitt and J. G. March, "Organizational learning," *Annual Review of Sociology*, vol. 14, pp. 516–540, 1988.
[73] J. G. March, "Exploration and exploitation in organizational learning," *Organization Science*, vol. 2, no. 1, pp. 71–87, 1991.
[74] D. Miller, "A preliminary typology of organizational learning: Synthesizing the literature," *Journal of Management*, vol. 22, no. 3, pp. 485–505, 1996.
[75] B. A. Ribbens, "Organizational learning styles: Categoring strategic predispositions from learning," *International Journal of Organizational Analysis*, vol. 5, no. 1, pp. 59–73, 1997.
[76] G. Romme, "Mapping the landscape of organizational learning," *European Management Journal*, vol. 15, no. 1, pp. 68–78, 1997.
[77] E. H. Schein, "Three cultures of management: The key to organizational learning," *Sloan Management Review*, vol. 38, no. 1, pp. 9–20, 1996.
[78] P. Shrivastava, "A typology of organizational learning systems," *The Journal of Management Studies*, vol. 20, no. 1, pp. 7–28, 1983.
[79] Simon, H. A. "Bounded rationality and organizational learning," *Organization Science*, vol. 2, no. 1, pp. 125–134, 1991.
[80] J. M. Sinkula, "A framework for market-based organizational learning: Linking values, knowledge, and behavior," *Academy of Marketing Science*, vol. 25, no. 4, pp. 305–318, 1997.
[81] E. W. K. Tsang, "Organizational learning and the learning organization: A dichotomy between descriptive and prescriptive research," *Human Relations*, vol. 50, no. 1, pp. 73–89, 1997.
[82] R. P. Winter, "Reframing managers' control orientations and practices: A proposed organizational learning framework," *International Journal of Organizational Analysis*, vol. 5, no. 1, pp. 9–24, 1997.
[83] H. G. Barkema, "Working abroad, working with others: How firms learn to operate international joint ventures," *Academy of Management Journal*, vol. 40, no. 2, pp. 426–442, 1997.
[84] D. J. Cyr and S. C. Schneider, "Implications for learning: Human resource management in east–west joint ventures," *Organization Studies*, vol. 17, no. 2, pp. 207–226, 1996.
[85] A. C. Inkpen and M. M. Crossan, "Believing is seeing: Joint ventures and organization learning," *Journal of Management Studies*, vol. 32, no. 5, pp. 595–618, 1995.
[86] B. Kogut, "Joint ventures: Theoretical and empirical perspectives," *Strategic Management Journal*, vol. 9, no. 4, pp. 319–332, 1988.
[87] M. A. Lyles, "Learning among joint venture sophisticated firms," *Management International Review*, vol. 28, Special Issue, pp. 85–98, 1988.
[88] M. V. Makhija, "The relationship between control and partner learning in learning-related joint ventures," *Organization Science*, vol. 8, no. 5, pp. 508–527, 1997.
[89] F.-J. Richter and K. Vettel, "Successful joint ventures in Japan: Transferring knowledge through organizational learning," *Long Range Planning*, vol. 28, no. 3, pp. 37–45, 1995.
[90] H. K. Steensma, "Acquiring technological competencies through inter-organization collaboration: An organizational learning perspective," *Journal of Engineering and Technology Management*, vol. 12, no. 4, pp. 267–286, 1996.

[91] P. S. Chan and A. Wong, "Global strategic alliances and organizational learning," *Leadership & Organization Development Journal*, vol. 15, no. 4, pp. 31–37, 1994.
[92] M. M. Crossan, "The subtle art of learning through alliances," *Ivey Business Quarterly*, vol. 60, no. 2, pp. 68–76, 1995.
[93] Y. L. Doz, "The evolution of cooperation in strategic alliances: Initial conditions or learning processes?" *Strategic Management Journal*, vol. 17, Special Issue, pp. 55–83, 1996.
[94] J. E. Gail, "Strategic alliances as 'virtual integration': A longitudinal exploration of biotech industry-level learning," *Academy of Management Journal*, Best Paper Proceedings, pp. 469–473, 1995.
[95] G. Hamel, "Competition for competence and inter-partner learning within international strategic alliances," *Strategic Management Journal*, vol. 12, Special Issue, pp. 83–103, 1991.
[96] A. Hjalager, "Interorganizational learning systems," *Human Systems Management*, vol. 18, no. 1, pp. 23–33, 1999.
[97] A. C. Inkpen, "Learning and knowledge acquisition through international strategic alliances," *The Academy of Management Executive*, vol. 12, no. 4, pp. 69–80, 1998.
[98] P. J. Lane, "Relative absorptive capacity and interorganizational learning," *Strategic Management Journal*, vol. 19, no. 5, pp. 461–477, 1998.
[99] R. Larsson, "The interorganizational learning dilemma: Collective knowledge development in strategic alliances," *Organization Science*, vol. 9, no. 3, pp. 285–305, 1998.
[100] D. Lei, "Building cooperative advantage: Managing strategic alliances to promote organizational learning," *Journal of World Business*, vol. 32, no. 3, pp. 203–223, 1997.
[101] N. S. Levinson, "Cross-national alliances and interorganizational learning," *Organizational Dynamics*, vol. 24, no. 2, pp. 50–63, 1995.
[102] D. C. Mowery, "Strategic alliances and interfirm knowledge transfer," *Strategic Management Journal*, vol. 17, pp. 77–91, Winter 1996.
[103] G. E. Osland and A. Yaprak, "Learning through strategic alliances: Processes and factors," *European Journal of Marketing*, vol. 29, no. 3, pp. 52–66, 1995.
[104] V. Pucik, "Strategic alliances, organizational learning, and competitive advantage: The HRM agenda," *Human Resource Management*, vol. 27, no. 1, pp. 77–93, 1988.

Knowledge Sharing Through Intranet-Based Learning: A Case Study of an Online Learning Center

Shan L. Pan
Department of Information Systems
School of Computing
National University of Singapore

Ming-Huei Hsieh
Helen Chen
Department of Marketing and Strategic Management
Warwick Business School
University of Warwick

Recent academic and managerial interest in electronic commerce (e-commerce) activities has created enormous interest in the world of information technology and in many other industries. Therefore, managers are facing new challenges. One such daunting task is the ability to manage knowledge, as this can now be exchanged or transferred on the Internet or Intranet without physical contact or time constraints. To understand some of the key human resource issues related to organizing global knowledge in the e-commerce context, an exploratory case study was conducted. One of the key findings from this case study is the recognition that human resource management (HRM) will play a new dual role in organizing global knowledge sharing in the e-commerce era. One role is to continue dealing with traditional administrative transactions and the other is to nurture knowledge-related activities. This contradicts simplistic prescriptions about managing knowledge, which suggests that the implementation and utilization of a particular information system are all that are necessary to facilitate effective knowledge sharing. Instead, this exploratory study shows that successful knowledge sharing is dependent not only on the use of particular information technologies but also on the successful creation of a knowledge-sharing environment with a knowledge management-focused HRM as the coordinator of related activities.

e-commerce, knowledge management, human resource management

We thank the guest editor, James Thong and the four anonymous reviewers for their helpful comments, which significantly enhanced the quality of the manuscript.

Correspondence and requests for reprints should be sent to Shan L. Pan, Department of Information Systems, School of Computing, National University of Singapore, 10 Kent Ridge Crescent, Singapore 119260. E-mail: Pansl@comp.nus.edu.sg

1. INTRODUCTION

Electronic commerce (e-commerce) is associated with technology as an enabler, facilitator, and even inhibitor of business activities both within and among all types of organizations [1]. It is thus creating enormous interest in the world of information technology (IT). There is little doubt that growth in this area will continue as more organizations join in, establishing and cultivating business relations, performing business transactions, distributing business knowledge, and implementing competition strategies [1]. Developing new business strategies has now become one of the most important challenges facing organizations in the era of e-commerce [2]. One such daunting task is the need to manage knowledge that can be exchanged or transferred on the Internet or Intranet without physical contacts or time constraints [3].

Knowledge has been identified as one of the most important resources that contribute to the competitive advantage of an organization [4]. This has led to a number of studies that have attempted to understand how an organization explores and exploits knowledge [4–6]. Despite the popularity of the notion of organizational knowledge and knowledge-intensive organizations (KIOs), relatively few studies have provided empirical insights into how companies manage their employees through the interplay between organizational contexts and IT [7]. Instead, some of the existing knowledge management (KM) literature has engaged in ontological debate about the nature of knowledge, and therefore tends to promote particular approaches as universal panaceas. More specifically, with the development of KM study, there has been a massive outpouring of articles and books (e.g., [8–10]) dealing with these issues from a prescriptive standpoint. Their relatively weak empirical base notwithstanding, many of these contributions confidently define organizational knowledge as a kind of economic asset or commodity, or as a purely cognitive phenomenon [11].

This study has selected ChemCo[1] for an in-depth study by addressing the gap between conceptual research and organizational practice. It aims at highlighting the human resource management (HRM) dimension by demonstrating the temporal interplay of three key factors proved critical in ChemCo's global KM (an online learning center) initiative (1996–1998), namely, training and performance measurement, rewards and incentives, and a new role for HRM. This article is arranged as follows: The first section reviews related literature. In the second section, the research methodology is presented, followed by an introduction of the case company and findings from the data analysis by examining the development of an online learning center. That section highlights the carefully managed interplay between KM-focused HRM and KM tools developed at ChemCo. Finally, three lessons that were learned from the case findings are shown.

2. A REVIEW OF RELATED LITERATURE

KM has enjoyed a rapid growth in the 1990s [6, 11, 12]. In the existing literature, there is certainly no shortage of opinions and theories about KM. The field of KM brings together a range of different issues, including the economies of knowledge

---

[1]ChemCo is a pseudonym; all names have been changed to ensure anonymity.

[13–15], the emergence of knowledge as an important resource [4, 14], learning [16], cognition [17, 18], and the taxonomy of knowledge [6, 19]. Although the field continues to show progress in understanding the nature of KM, most of the existing studies suffer from unintegrated efforts that are the result of "methodological manoeuvres institutionalized into the contemporary analysis of organizational knowledge"([17], p. 66).

In the context of the e-commerce era, existing literature has shown that the focus of KM studies has moved from knowledge to the process of knowing activities taking place in virtual communities [6, 12]. Particularly in these days when IT has facilitated the formation of many virtual communities [20], it is worthwhile examining KM in the context of e-commerce.

In addition, as we can see, very few studies to date have examined the so-called KIOs. Even in some of the rare cases, they are often described as organizations staffed by a high proportion of highly qualified staff who trade in knowledge itself [7, 21]. We know comparatively little about the actual organizational processes through which knowledge is valued in competitive outcomes [22] using advanced technologies in a global manner. At the same time, the absence of an understanding for managing knowledge workers on a broad, global, and relevant basis becomes an increasingly critical problem for managers. In particular, the details of a KM-focused HRM are rarely discussed in existing studies. This is perhaps due to the general lack of empirical studies of KM [23].

Against such a backdrop, this exploratory study departs on a perspective that has been previously suggested by Scarbrough [24] in describing the nature of knowledge work. According to him, "knowledge work is less a matter of the application of predefined expertise and more a joint product of human interactions with informational and intellectual assets delivered through information and communication technologies" (p. 7). Therefore, in this research, processes of KM are integrated into the fabric of the organization, thus requiring a conceptual shift away from the traditional view of the company. As such, traditional managerial activities that focus on the improvement of human relationships, communications, group and team processes, and performance evaluation and improvement now take on new interpretations and meanings due to the employment of e-commerce, thereby reconceptualizing the role of HRM.

Therefore, the case study aims to demonstrate the development of an online learning center being part of a much wider debate about the shifting demands of the importance of knowledge and sources of competitiveness in the era of e-commerce. Such beliefs are reflected in the current interest in KM, which has raised a number of questions about the ways that IT and knowledge workers are managed.

3. RESEARCH DESIGN

This article is based on a detailed case study of ChemCo. The research adopted a retrospective approach. The main fieldwork was conducted on-site at ChemCo's corporate headquarters, with semistructured interviews carried out with the most knowledgeable managers [25] and informants. Informants were encouraged to express things in their own terminology and experiences. To provide a managerial perspective as well as a holistic organizational perspective, the researcher formally interviewed 12 top managers (including the chairman and chief executive officer of the company) and 38 other employees. The range of interviewees covered the different actors and management levels involved in the development and implementation processes.

The first step in the data collection process involved gaining access to ChemCo by contacting its top management to solicit participation. Given the difficulties in gaining access, the researcher resorted to a relation model and maintained flexible entry tactics and strategies [26]. Through reviews of the literature, ChemCo was identified as a potential case company for in-depth study. The overall strategy of gaining access was twofold. First, the immediate aim was to identify key players in the context of KM initiatives. Taking a rather different approach from the "contacting middle management" strategy proposed by Buchanan et al. [27], an e-mail was first sent to the chairman of the company—the *gatekeeper*, to use Becker's [28] term—expressing an interest in learning more about ChemCo's KM experience. Then, after a preliminary study of the company was made, access issues were proposed and negotiated.

Initially, in the early stage of the preliminary study, some e-mails were exchanged with the chairman and a "snowball" sampling method was applied to generate a list of key guides and informants for further contacts. After the initial contacts with the chairman, 15 employees were selected by the chairman for the first stage of the study, including either the chairman or a member of the top management team and the knowledge transfer department vice-president. In total, during this phase, unstructured interviews and discussions through a total of 150 e-mails were conducted. Although the strategy of obtaining an initial list of potential interviewees from the chairman might be seen as biased and problematic, this list of names was used as a starting point rather than as a final, definitive guide to research. Moreover, the suggested list was triangulated via multiple checking to assess whether they were seen as representative by other interviewees.

Observations of meetings, training classes, and individuals at work were also made throughout the study. The field notes from these observations were used to verify or elaborate the interview data. In addition, access to the case company's Intranet was gained. The company supplied a laptop, allowing observation of knowledge transfer in real time during the site visit. More than 50 online discussions over global KM issues were also carried out with employees from Europe, Asia, and Latin America to provide insights into the complex cross-cultural social and technical issues around managing global knowledge. In addition, eight KM-related meetings were attended and observed. Five telephone interviews and over 200 e-mail interviews were conducted to collect and verify data. The technical details of the knowledge-sharing systems were provided mainly through archival data. Documentary evidence permitted crosschecking of much of the interview materials. It was possible to verify the reliability of managers' recollections on technical and other details by comparing them with internal documents. Interpretation of empirical events was furthered through discussions with the other members of the research group and several KM researchers and practitioners outside the case company. The use of externally oriented articles provided yet another possibility to triangulate the validity of the interview data. In addition to interviews, observations, archival material, and supplemental data collection and member checks were applied. Specifically, archival data was collected in the form of newsletters, handbooks, vignettes, and instructional videos produced by ChemCo or from information held on ChemCo's Intranet.

The collected data was analyzed systematically based on concepts of open coding, axial coding, and selective coding [29]. Iteration between data and concepts helped the researcher to generate categories and subcategories, and identify potential links between categories. Drawing on the analytical technique proposed by Miles and Huberman [30], patterns that were unique to one case or applicable to the two cases were identified through matrix displays. Such pattern-matching processes enabled the researcher to enhance the internal validity of the research findings [31]. One process that was interwoven with the data analysis and interpretation was literature comparison. The purpose of drawing intensively on the current literature was to compare the emergent theory with similar theories and also to contrast it with conflicting literature to ensure internal validity [32]. In addition, literature comparison served as a vital source of theoretical creativity [33].

3.1 Case Background and Analysis

ChemCo is a $300 million (annual turnover) chemical company, serving industries in 102 countries, selling 1,000 different specialist chemicals. It was established in 1945 as a manufacturer of specialist chemicals for aqueous industrial systems. Triggered by increasing external competition in 1989, the management decided that knowledge would become the foundation of the company's competitive edge. Three years later, the implementation of the K'Netix® knowledge network marked the realization of that vision.

By 1993, for a total of $75,000 (U.S. dollars) per month in access charges and an IBM ThinkPad 720 (IBM, White Plains, NY) with a modem, all ChemCo employees could make a single phone call to establish a point-to-point with headquarters and provide necessary access to global information services. Based on the concept, K'Netix® was introduced with seven forums (three customer-focused forums and four regional-focused forums) established to coordinate ChemCo's online conversations (for the development of ChemCo's Learning Center initiative since 1992, see Table 1).

In 1996, apart from continuously providing infrastructure for systematic knowledge sharing, the ChemCo management decided to create a multilingual, online learning center for human resource development (HRD) as part of the KM-focused HRM strategy. Building on its maturing ICT platform and knowledge-sharing environment, the company began experimenting in 1996 with Lotus's novel educational product LearningSpace™. This allowed employees to increase their knowledge through Intranet-based learning and training. It also helped to keep track of customer service calls and needs.

Prior to this experiment, ChemCo had produced computer-based training (CBT) programs in 1992 to provide self-paced, anytime, anywhere, course materials to their employees. These programs were produced on a course-by-course basis. In 1995, the Distance Learning Team was formed to expand and centralize distance-learning efforts. This group laid the foundation for the ChemCo Learning Center, which was set up to coordinate the delivery and administration of electron-

Table 1
The Development of Knowledge Transfer and Learning Center Initiatives Since 1992

Year	Major Events
1992	The start of global knowledge transfer initiative; computer-based training was introduced
1993 to 1995	The establishments of regional discussion forums; distance learning courses provided to all employees
1996	Began experiment with Lotus LearningSpace™; launch of the online Learning Center
1997 to 1998	Toward incorporating Learning Center activities as part of knowledge management-based human resource management

ically distributed educational and training programs for the personal and professional development of employees. It encompasses learning opportunities ranging from short training courses to advanced academic degrees.

The original purposes behind ChemCo's distance learning efforts included the need to reduce the duplication of training efforts among technical experts and the need to make training consistent across associate companies. The use of CBT to train employees has provided the company with a sales force that is better prepared to solve customers' problems. It has also

- Enhanced learning and training opportunities
- Reduced training time for new recruits
- Empowered employees to engage in personal and career development
- Created a knowledge advantage over competitors
- Produced a value-added benefit to sell to customers
- Ensured globally standardized training
- Reduced time away from customers

To deliver these benefits to employees, the development of the ChemCo Learning Center was linked to three primary goals. The first was to provide a coordinated training and development function within ChemCo. The second was to apply the available technologies to deliver training and development efforts in a cost-effective way. Third, the Learning Center was to play a critical role in keeping employees up to date with their profession [34]. To make the objectives of the Learning Center clear, a mission statement was created, which focused on the success and development of employees:

> The ChemCo Learning Center supports the corporate mission by delivering, developing, and facilitating world class training and educational opportunities, when and where they are needed. We empower employees to manage their personal and career development, create competitive market advantage and engage customers with our products and services. [34]

One of the key elements in establishing the Learning Center was the use of ICT for global information and knowledge dissemination. The use of computers in employee training and learning is considered by some researchers as both cost effective and a powerful learning method. The choice of ICT for the center has implications for the cost and convenience of the existing Intranet system. According to one computer engineer at the center:

> Because the responsibility of the learning center is to provide and deliver learning opportunities, the infrastructure should be built alongside the existing system—that way it could ensure minimum systems training and time spent on design and technical issues.

As a result, tools such as Lotus's Domino™ and Microsoft's FrontPage™ were used to facilitate design and content modification (note that Lotus Domino™ is an integrated messaging and Web application software platform for companies that need to improve customer responsiveness and streamline business processes. Microsoft FrontPage™ is a Web site creation and management tool).

The decision to use these particular forms of software was also driven by the central belief that in using IT, content and learning objectives should drive the technology employed, and not vice versa.

Once the choice of software was made, the Learning Center project team had to decide on the issue of delivery options. The team had to choose between asynchronous, synchronous, and instructor interaction. The key factor in making this decision was the type of content to be delivered. As the director of the center put it, "Given the dispersed nature of our employees, our bias has been the choice of asynchronous delivery tools over our corporate Intranet." Asynchronous Internet-based training was selected and facilitated through the use of tools such as Lotus Notes® and LearningSpace™, learning within the environment of virtual collaboration. The cost and speed of distribution are always important issues in relation to virtual training delivery. According to one computer engineer, the main advantage of using asynchronous Internet-based training is that many of the courses offered are text-downloaded asynchronously and that it tends to use less access bandwidth than the real-time instruction approach. On the other hand, real-time communication requires more capacity. The bandwidth availability required by offering real-time courses might also limit the type of courses to be offered. Another reason for not choosing the real-time option is that it would restrict the availability of employees for training.

In 1998, although the scheme was still in its very early stages, more and more ChemCo employees were signing up for the virtual learning center courses. The center has begun to provide continuous training and learning for the communities of practice (CoP) that form around issues and then disband when those issues are resolved. It is widely believed at ChemCo that all future training of workers working in a knowledge-intensive environment is likely to be conducted via Internet-based or other computer-based alternatives.

3.2 Online Training

As already mentioned, one major task of the Learning Center was to provide job-related training via the company's Intranet. Some employees regarded this as a natural development:

> An evolutionary step from traditional training departments is the growing realisation and acceptance that learning need not happen in a centralised location in front of an instructor. (Director of the Learning Center)

Not only did the sales employees welcome the initiatives, nontechnical staff members were also excited, as they had not previously been offered any opportunities for further learning. As one nontechnical associate commented,

> For non-sales employees learning is left to ourselves. I have not in five years been on a further training or education course specific to my job funded by ChemCo. This may be available if I asked, but I have never been informed of a further education programme being available to employees. To support the front-line I do ensure I read and learn, as much as time allow, information on new products new applications etc, and regularly read forums to gain knowledge by osmosis. This on-line learning is a great news for me. (Internal survey, 1995)

Despite the groundbreaking efforts in establishing online learning and training programs, not all ChemCo employees were convinced by the function of the ChemCo Learning Center:

> We need to do a better job of hands-on learning and "mentoring" in field applications. All the access in the world won't help if the representative does not know what question to ask. (Internal survey, 1995)

To address some of the concerns relating to the establishment of the new Learning Center, it was made clear to ChemCo employees that the philosophy of the center went beyond the traditional notions of classroom and teacher. It was developed as the organization's response to changing external circumstances as well as being part of the continuous global knowledge-sharing initiative. As the director of the Learning Center explained

> The ChemCo Learning Center is founded on two basic strategic assumptions. First, that ChemCo's competitive advantage resides in the collective knowledge of its employees, and second, to sustain that advantage the company must invest in the skills and competencies of our employees. (Director of the Learning Center, 1998)

Still in its very early stages, the ChemCo Learning Center's efforts have been focused on increasing the knowledge of each associate. In particular, the focus of the center was on researching and acquiring the necessary training materials. To that end, since 1997, ChemCo's Learning Center has been working with content providers such as universities from specific geographical areas to enhance the flexibility of its training courses. As one director at the learning center noted

> We're also offering the ability for our translation group to partner with certain content providers to actually translate their existing content and the determine how we could barter that service back into advantages for the content provider as well, because then, we could effectively provide them with a translated copy of their material and expect something in return. (Director of the Learning Center, 1998)

The content provided was drawn from some of the best universities in the world as well as from custom-designed tools to help with employees' day-to-day duties. Content and direction were driven by the needs of ChemCo employees:

> The current goals include fully automated on-line administration of all training within the world-wide company, full language translation (into English, Spanish, Portuguese, French, and German), personalisation of curricula, skill set gap analysis, etc. As this is a new venture, we are still in the process of formulating many of our long-term goals. (Informant from the Learning Center, 1998)

3.3 Slowness in Deploying a Systematic KM-Focused HRM

Despite ChemCo's concerted efforts to provide HRD activities online, the need for innovation in systematic and organization-wide KM-focused HRM—involving the design of new training programs, performance evaluation and reward systems, and the introduction of knowledge leadership—soon become apparent. This was clearly evident in a comment made by one sales person in an internal survey:

> The training has in the past been given by KTD (knowledge transfer department), who do a good job at the "this is how it works" approach. But we need to focus much more on what benefits can be obtained from sharing knowledge. One option might be to train a few sales people, let them be involved in documenting the benefits, using case history data in the training materials etc and selling the KM concept to the rest of the sales team, using KM department as training facilitators.

Part of the call for a systematic KM-focused HRM was the need for a reward and incentive system. Since 1992, ChemCo has occasionally introduced incentive programs to build enthusiasm and momentum around the principles of KM. When KM was first introduced in 1992, as indicated earlier, there was some resistance toward the initiative. One of the possible reasons for this was the lack of employee motivation. The main source of the problem, as explained by one research and development scientist, was the fear of job insecurity in relation to the sharing of personal knowledge:

> Compensate the experts to give their knowledge to others. Where is the incentive for the experts to give their knowledge to others and then be replaced by computer data in the future! They are not going to participate and cut their own career.

To overcome this, a series of innovative approaches was used to encourage participation. An example was provided and explained by a former forum specialist: "There was a sense of resistance in the beginning, what we did was to mix a reward-and-punishment approach." Accordingly, a number of incentives were offered at the level of the individual:

> Once in a while, we gave out monetary rewards ($50) for our Latin employees for their contributions in knowledge sharing. With the culture there, US dollars are always an incentive. Together with certificates, the monetary rewards were considered as suc-

cesses, and it was later observed that participation in knowledge sharing there has gone up.

Although ChemCo does not offer regular financial rewards for posting knowledge, selective rewards have been utilized from time to time. For example, a one-time event at a fashionable resort was arranged for the 150 employees who had contributed the most widely used knowledge. At this event, employees helped to shape the future of the KM initiatives. Those chosen received new laptop computers and participated in a number of KM-related discussions. However, this less than scientific approach to taking decisions met with some criticism:

> There was a lot of resentment in the company about how people were chosen and what was going on. That lasted and is still present and so I think there's still a lot of resentment toward KTD just for that reason. You know, because everyone who was there got a brand new computer was rewarded and recognized. I think in some ways the resentment kept people from participating later. (Marketing Manager)

Although some of those not included in the event felt disappointed and unhappy, the overall level of participation in the knowledge-sharing forums rose immediately. At the same time, the punishment component became more subtle but even more persuasive. For example, during the early implementation period of K'Netix®, top management wrote to employees who did not participate in the sharing activities. The management asked why they did not wish to contribute, stressing that previous ways of working were becoming defunct and that change was necessary to secure the organization's future success. Some of the reasons cited were related to being uncomfortable with technological changes and job insecurity issues. These concerns were taken aboard by the top management and played a big role in their subsequent development and implementation of KM-focused HRM.

Although recognizing the importance of having a systemic evaluation and rewards system and performance measurement system for knowledge sharing, ChemCo did not begin to consider such needs seriously until 1997. The issue of knowledge worker performance measurement remains one of the most important yet least developed aspects of ChemCo's efforts to organize knowledge sharing. As one informant explained,

> We are just now (after seven years of implementing knowledge sharing) in a process of developing standardized job profiles for all of our employees which all contain a list of performance skills in addition to whatever other ones they need in their particular positions.

The slowness in developing a systematic KM-focused HRM was due to the fact that ChemCo management initially felt that focusing too much on knowledge itself might actually hinder the normal process of knowledge dissemination, according to a vice president of human resources. To avoid that, "a valuable alternative implemented is the measurement and monitoring of both the process improvement and related outcomes." However, this proved to be insufficient as more and more employees were expecting clearer performance measurement details.

When ChemCo embraced the concept of KM in the early 1990s, top management knew it would take more than sophisticated technology and leading edge software to promote coherence and ensure success. To be precise, managers at ChemCo believed that it would take the following three key factors to implement KM successfully: advanced KM systems and tools, continuous cultural change, and KM-focused HRM. These knowledge-sharing initiatives were both planned and allowed to emerge over time, thus allowing sufficient flexibility to respond to unforeseeable changes in the internal and external environments. Based on the case findings, the following section aims to draw out some lessons that could have future implications and are worthy of future research.

3.4 Lessons Learned: Toward a New Role for HRM

In view of the trends toward virtual community-based organization and human-centered implementation of KM, HRM at ChemCo has moved increasingly toward playing a coordinating role in aligning knowledge activities behind common purposes, norms, and values.

Our interpretation of ChemCo's experience in its learning center raises several interesting future research implications for other organizations. In the following section, the study aims to present descriptive findings on the lessons learned and provide a number of possible questions for further research in this area. The lessons learned from the case study are the following: the provision of training and performance evaluation, rewards and incentives, and the new role for HRM.

4. TRAINING AND PERFORMANCE MEASUREMENT

One of the major requirements for an effective development of a KM-focused HRM is related to the training and performance evaluation of knowledge workers. Traditional organizations have considered training as an expense to be minimized. This is also the fundamental reason why organizations generally prefer to hire ready-trained workers rather than provide training themselves [35, 36]. However, as the nature of work-related knowledge becomes more fluid, organizations have no choice but to take training needs more seriously. To become more efficient in providing training for employees, more and more organizations are beginning to adopt the strategy of just-in-time learning via the Internet or Intranet [37].

With the trend toward providing flexible training using ICT, HR managers are likely to take on two additional training responsibilities in managing knowledge workers: to provide training in an online knowledge-intensive environment and provide KM-focused HRM activities. Brown [38] emphasized the key role of HR specialists in new interpretative communities through the provision of training experiences that can develop the ability to contribute to constructive knowledge sharing. This implies that training is to be provided online in and across CoPs. In other words, it suggests that knowledge should be acquired when and where it is needed. In this regard, in addition to the traditional distance learning concept, a number of emerging practices in promoting just-in-time learning are now being adopted by organizations, including the following: cross-training by coworkers, job rotation, suggestions systems, skill-based pay, and formal or informal groups

[37]. The last two practices are particularly important in the case of ChemCo's own experience in developing its online learning center.

Another immediate implication for HRM is the adoption of KM-focused training and personnel development. In terms of knowledge-sharing training at ChemCo, HR personnel were left out of the decision-making and implementation process almost entirely, at least in the initial stage. Most KM-related training was left to the KTD Department. Only recently (1998) did HR personnel begin to work with KTD personnel in developing training materials for knowledge sharing as well as for other job-related training. This involves allowing greater flexibility in employees' use of time so that they can adjust to the new technologies of KM tools. For example, employees are encouraged to learn how to use the ICT-based knowledge transfer system, to understand the system's short-term and long-term benefits, and to review its effectiveness (e.g., in terms of facilitating knowledge sharing).

In fact, the lack of systematic evaluation and expectation of employees' participation in knowledge sharing is one important reason why ChemCo did not become a truly knowledge-intensive firm earlier. Among the obstacles to such an innovation, one key factor was the nature of a knowledge worker's job, which is extremely varied, complex, and often highly individualistic. However, in due course, the company appreciated that, given its reliance on the contributions made by knowledge workers, meaningful performance measurement through qualitative practices was essential as a mechanism for motivating their work and facilitating knowledge sharing in the CoPs. The qualitative practices include a number of contributions to internal practice databases, internal coaching and mentoring, effective team working and team development, and product innovation. In this way, skill- and knowledge-based performance evaluation systems, which are a major departure from traditional HRM practices, have become the core of the performance evaluation system at ChemCo.

5. REWARDS AND INCENTIVES

Any discussion of the issue of performance measurement inevitably requires an examination of the use of rewards and incentives. In general, the rise in the number and importance of knowledge workers is changing the balance of power within organizations and creating new tensions and responsibilities between management and knowledge workers. In this case, ChemCo employees no longer work only for financial incentives and packages. Instead, the notion of incentive-based knowledge sharing has been implemented as part of the company's knowledge-sharing culture.

Since the beginning of the implementation, ChemCo managers have been using "creative incentives" to encourage knowledge workers to participate in knowledge sharing ([39], p. 694). Usually, these have been in the form of compensation and rewards and have been linked to the factors that help to improve the level of participation within the organization. Use has also been made of one-time rewards. For example, in 1994, 150 ChemCo employees were selected to participate in a meeting held at a holiday resort in the United States, and they were all given new laptop computers to encourage their active participation in sharing knowledge.

Although the use of rewards was recognized as an effective management tool for the encouragement of key knowledge-sharing behaviors at ChemCo, it was also seen to be double edged. This is because it generated resistance among some employees, particularly because it was linked to explicit sanctions for those who were less willing to cooperate. Despite the difficulties, however, the reward practice at ChemCo succeeded in establishing the principle that employees should be rewarded according to their knowledge contribution instead of their formal job titles. This has undoubtedly provided concrete incentives for ChemCo employees to share knowledge within the organization. However, the use of rewards and incentives has been sporadic and ad hoc rather than systematic.

What the study suggests is that the use of incentives and rewards in organizing knowledge sharing needs to be part of a comprehensive knowledge culture-building effort. It is extremely important to create a context in which knowledge sharing is encouraged or even demanded. Therefore, there is a need to foster a climate in which there is a powerful social obligation to share. Ultimately, it is a HR task to provide appropriate training, both technical and nontechnical, for knowledge workers. It is clear from the case study that knowledge-based compensation and reward schemes focused on challenges inherent in the nature of knowledge work while ensuring that monetary rewards and their administration never became an issue for knowledge workers. Therefore, the new focus of compensation in organizations needs to shift from old organizing models to new ones that are tailored to the exigencies of knowledge work [40].

6. THE DEVELOPMENT OF A KM-FOCUSED HRM

Finally, as far as developing a KM-focused HRM is concerned, there can be no doubt that the management of HR and competency is a crucial issue in organizing knowledge sharing. Keegan [41] used a detailed study of people management in a knowledge-intensive firm to demonstrate that traditional HRM practice prescription does not fit the needs of knowledge-intensive firms. The case study findings support Keegan's findings, while adding that a KM-focused HRM is probably best developed after the initial stages of the knowledge-sharing system have been implemented.

In the case study, one of ChemCo's vital ingredients for the success of knowledge sharing was identified as its interrelation with HRM. Traditionally, the HR department was responsible for training and education, career development, and making available and developing appropriate HRs. With the growing emphasis on the importance of knowledge, the role of the department inevitably changed. For example, since 1996, the Learning Center has been developed with an emphasis on allowing its employees to manage their personal and career development and bringing new knowledge and skills to its employees in a cost-effective manner. Such change implies a new role for HRM with major organizational implications for HR managers [40]. In this case, the challenge facing HR managers is to facilitate a balance between the macro considerations, such as structural groups and cultural norms, and micro considerations, including a whole range of personnel practices and standards [42].

This study provides important empirical evidence and lessons on how a KM-focused HRM was coordinated in an effort to organize knowledge sharing. First, the findings highlight the contribution of specific HRD that help provide training and development initiatives for knowledge workers. As evidenced in the case study, HRD is being delivered in novel ways (e.g., through the development of the online ChemCo Learning Center). HRD support of this kind is important not only in providing specific kinds of training and information, but also in promoting a common language and understanding among participants in CoPs [43].

Second, the coordinating role of HR in facilitating knowledge sharing has also provided exciting opportunities for ChemCo employees to nurture, shape, and transform the CoPs with the assistance of the ICT-based knowledge transfer system. With the new responsibilities of HR managers, a KM-focused HRM may be seen to have two major roles: one in dealing with traditional administrative transactions, and the other in nurturing knowledge-related activities. ChemCo's KM-focused HR teams have undertaken these roles by inserting influences without authority, building bridges, coordinating activities between information technologists and members of CoPs, and viewing themselves as catalysts.

Third, the case findings also imply that HRM should move beyond a narrow focus on training to take a more central role in coordinating the context (social and technical) that facilitates knowledge sharing. Such a shift in perspective requires the ability to provide meaningful systematic measurement indicators and to contribute to constructive dialogue. In this regard, ChemCo's experience suggests that the measurement of the benefits and results of knowledge sharing alone was not the highest priority in organizing knowledge sharing. It was more productive in the early stages to observe, monitor, nurture, and celebrate early success than to work out elaborate knowledge-related measures.

Finally, as emerged from the case study, the following questions deserve further attention in future research:

- What kinds of information systems are best for conducting online training activities?
- How would online training be different from other forms of training, in terms of the ability to manage knowledge in the e-commerce era?
- How should an organization evaluate online knowledge-sharing performance?
- How should knowledge workers be compensated? How are they different from existing rewards and incentives?
- Should incentive-based knowledge sharing be part of an organization culture?
- How should an incentive-based global knowledge-sharing system be implemented?
- Should HR take on the challenges of facilitating global knowledge sharing? Or, is it something that top management or the IT department should take on?
- What new IT skills are needed for HR to play a proactive role in the 21st century?

7. CONCLUSIONS

Managing knowledge has become the most challenging task facing managers in today's e-commerce era. As mentioned earlier, with the new IT (such as Internet and

Intranet), knowledge sharing and learning can be rearranged, HRM redirected, and customer service reshaped. In particular, the ability to deal with the sociotechnical interactions of IT and social elements involved in managing knowledge has been highlighted in the case study.

The need for a KM-focused HRM is recognized not just as a simple implementation issue, but as an indication that a fuller understanding of the KM-focused HRM policies and system design is necessary. HRM is probably the least developed aspect of the KM practices at ChemCo. Although management believed that the early introduction of knowledge-sharing performance measurement would hinder development, since 1998 it has moved toward developing systematic measurement systems. Therefore, as suggested in the case study, the compensation package for knowledge workers is shifting from objective and rational, toward subjective performance measures.

On the other hand, one of the most important findings from this exploratory case study was how HRM will play a new role in organizing global knowledge sharing in the e-commerce era. This contradicts the simplistic prescriptions about KM, which suggest that the implementation and utilization of a particular information system are all that is necessary to facilitate effective knowledge sharing [44]. Instead, this case study shows that successful knowledge sharing is dependent not only on the use of particular information technologies but also on the successful creation of a knowledge-sharing environment with a KM-focused HRM as the coordinator of related activities.

It is also worth pointing out that the failure to implement KM-focused HRM in most situations is not due to the inability to understand its benefits and importance to the organizations. Rather, it is often an organizational challenge that requires a comprehensive and sometimes complex change of mindset and environment. This perhaps explains why many innovative ideas for change often stop at the feasibility study level and rarely get implemented successfully.

Finally, the findings conclude that KIOs can be clearly distinguished by their flatter organization structures and decentralized decision-making processes. Managing these organizations is therefore different from managing traditional hierarchical organizations. At their core lies a particular knowledge-intensive thinking that concentrates specifically on intellect and reflection. Processes of KM are integrated into the fabric of the organization, thus requiring a conceptual shift away from the traditional view of the firm. As such, traditional managerial activities that focus on the improvement of human relations, communications, group and team processes, and performance evaluation and improvement, now take on new interpretations and meanings, thereby reconceptualizing the role of HRM.

REFERENCES

[1] L. M. Applegate, C. W. Holsapple, R. Kalakota, F. J. Radermacher, and A. B. Whinston, "Electronic commerce: Building blocks of new business opportunity," *Journal of Organizational Computing and Electronic Commerce*, vol. 6, no. 1, pp. 1–10, 1996.

[2] M. Bloch, Y. Pigneur, and A. Segev, "On the road of electronic commerce—A business value framework, gaining competitive advantage and some research issues," [Retrieved Jan. 5, 2000]. Available: www.stern.nyu.edu/~mbloch/docs/roadtoec/ec.htm

[3] P. Berthon, N. Lane, L. Pitt, and R. T. Watson, "The World Wide Web as an industrial marketing communication tool: Models for the identification and assessment of opportunities," *Journal of Marketing Management*, vol. 14, no. 7, pp. 691–704, 1998.

[4] R. Grant, "Toward a knowledge-based theory of the firm," *Strategic Management Journal*, vol. 17, pp. 109–122, Winter 1996.

[5] D. Leonard-Barton, "The factory as a learning laboratory," *Sloan Management Review*, vol. 34, pp. 23–38, Fall 1992.

[6] I. Nonaka and H. Takeuchi, *The Knowledge Creating Company*. New York: Oxford University Press, 1995.

[7] W. Starbuck, "Learning by knowledge-intensive firms," *Journal of Management Studies*, vol. 29, no. 6, pp. 713–740, 1992.

[8] P. Quintas, P. Lefrere, and G. Jones, "Knowledge management: A strategic agenda," *Long Range Planning*, vol. 30, no. 3, pp. 385–391, 1997.

[9] T. Stewart, *Intellectual Capital: The New Wealth of Organizations*. London: Brealey, 1997.

[10] T. Davenport and L. Prusak, *Working Knowledge: How Organizations Manage What They Know*. Boston, MA: Harvard Business School, 1998.

[11] S.-L. Pan and H. Scarbrough, "Knowledge management in practice: An exploratory case study," *Technology Analysis and Strategic Management*, vol. 11, no. 3, pp. 359–374, 1999.

[12] J. Brown and P. Deguid, "Organizational learning and communities-of-practice: Toward a unified view of working, learning, and innovation," *Organizational Science*, vol. 2, no. 1, pp. 40–57, 1991.

[13] P. Drucker, "The new society of organizations," *Harvard Business Review*, pp. 95–104, Sept.–Oct. 1992.

[14] C. Handy, *The Age of Unreason*. London: Arrow, 1989.

[15] T. Peters, "Thriving chaos," *Working Woman*, vol. 18, no. 9, pp. 42–45, 1993.

[16] P. M. Senge, *The Fifth Discipline*. New York: Doubleday, 1990.

[17] J.-C. Spender, "Making knowledge the basis of a dynamic theory of the firm," *Strategic Management Journal*, Special Issue, vol. 17, pp. 45–62, Winter 1996.

[18] J. Walsh and G. Ungson, "Organizational memory," *Academy of Management Review*, vol. 16, no. 3, pp. 57–91, 1991.

[19] M. Polanyi, *The Tacit Dimension*. New York: Anchor, 1966.

[20] M. Bloch, Y. Pigneur, and A. Segev, "On the road of electronic commerce—A business value framework, gaining competitive advantage and some research issues," (Retrieved Jan. 5, 2000). Available: www.stern.nyu.edu/~mbloch/docs/roadtoec/ec.htm

[21] M. Alvesson, "Organizations as rhetoric: Knowledge intensive firms and the struggle with ambiguity," *Journal of Management Studies*, vol. 30, no. 6, pp. 997–1015, 1993.

[22] G. Huber, "Organizational learning: The contributing processes and the literatures," *Organization Science*, vol. 2, no. 1, pp. 88–116, 1991.

[23] D. E. Leidner, "Information technology and organizational culture," in *Strategic Information Management*, R. D. Galliers, D. E. Leidner, and B. S. H. Baker, Eds. Oxford, England: Butterworth-Heinemann, 1999, pp. 523–550.

[24] H. Scarbrough, "Knowledge as work: Conflicts in the management of knowledge workers," *Technology Analysis & Strategic Management*, vol. 11, no. 1, pp. 5–16, 1999.

[25] G. P. Huber and D. J. Power, "Retrospective reports of strategic-level managers: Guidelines for increasing their accuracy," *Strategic Management Journal*, vol. 6, no. 2, pp. 171–180, 1985.

[26] W. Shaffir, R. A. Stebbins, and A. Turowetz, *Fieldwork Experience: Qualitative Approaches to Social Research*. New York: St. Martin, 1980.

[27] D. Buchanan, D. Boddy, and J. McCalman, "Getting in, getting on, getting out, and getting back," in *Doing Research in Organizations*, A. Bryman, Ed. London: Routledge, 1988.

[28] H. S. Becker, *Sociological Work: Method and Substance*. Chicago: Aldine, 1970.

[29] A. Strauss and J. Corbin, *Basics of Qualitative Research: Grounded Theory Procedures and Techniques*. London: Sage, 1990.

[30] M. B. Miles and A. M. Huberman, *Qualitative Data Analysis: A Sourcebook of New Methods*. Thousand Oaks, CA: Sage, 1994.

[31] R. Yin, *Case Study Research: Design and Methods* (2nd ed.). London: Sage, 1994.

[32] K. M. Eisehardt, "Making fast strategic decisions in high-velocity environments," *Academy of Management Journal*, vol. 32, no. 3, pp. 543–576, 1989.

[33] K. Weick, "Cognitive processes in organizations," *Research in Organizational Behaviour*, vol. 1, pp. 41–74, 1979.
[34] S. Ellis, "Buckman learning center," *Journal of Knowledge Management*, vol. 1, no. 3, pp. 189–196, 1998.
[35] L. M. Lynch, "Introduction," in *Training and the Private Sector: International Comparisons*, L. M. Lynch, Ed. Chicago: University of Chicago Press, 1994.
[36] D. Stern and J. M. M. Ritzen, *Market Failure in Training? New Economic Analysis and Evidence on Training of Adult Employees*. New York: Springer-Verlag, 1991.
[37] D. Stern, "Human resource development in the knowledge-based economy: Roles of firms, schools, and governments," in *The Knowledge Economy*, D. Neef, Ed. Boston: Butterworth-Heinemann, 1998, pp. 249–265.
[38] G. Brown, "Accounts, meaning and causality" in *Accounts and Actions*, G. Gilbert and P. Abell, Eds. Aldershot, England: Gower, 1984, pp. 21–31.
[39] S. Matusik and C. Hill, "The utilization of contingent work, knowledge creation, and competitive advantage," *Academy of Management Review*, vol. 23, no. 4, pp. 680–697, 1998.
[40] C. Despres and J.-M. Hiltrop, "Compensation for technical professionals in the knowledge age," *Research Technology Management*, vol. 39, pp. 49–56, Sept.–Oct. 1996.
[41] A. Keegan, "Management practice in knowledge-intensive firms: The future of HRM in the knowledge era," presented at British Academy of Management Conf., Nottingham, Sept. 1998.
[42] H. Bahrami and S. Evans, "Human resource leadership in knowledge-based entities: Shaping the context of work," *Human Resource Management*, vol. 36, no. 1, pp. 23–28, 1997.
[43] H. Scarbrough, "Conclusion: The concept of knowledge management," in *Case Studies in Knowledge Management*, H. Scarbrough and J. Swan, Eds. London: Institute of Personnel Development, 1999, pp. 85–93.
[44] D. Hislop, "The Movex project: Knowledge management at BrightCo," in *Case Studies in Knowledge Management*, H. Scarbrough and J. Swan, Eds. London: Institute of Personnel Development, 1999, pp. 51–58.

Internet Diffusion in Creative Micro-Businesses: Identifying Change Agent Characteristics As Critical Success Factors

Pascale de Berranger
David Tucker
Laurie Jones
*The Business School
Department of Business Information Technology
Manchester Metropolitan University*

Micro-businesses make a substantial contribution to the economic and social well being of Europe, the Asian Pacific region, and the United States. In Europe, for example, 30% of firms with less than 10 employees generate 70% of turnover. This remarkable statistic has prompted the European Union to fund novel research projects aimed at stimulating growth within the very small businesses sector. In particular, projects aimed at improving the adoption rate of information and communication technology (ICT) are seen as vital. The Internet is a unique and powerful form of ICT, which is making electronic commerce attractive to even the smallest of businesses. These micro-businesses stand to gain tremendous business advantages from implementing Internet technology. For this reason, in this article we focus specifically on Internet diffusion processes in micro-businesses.[1] Through a field study within a geographic cluster of creative micro-businesses, we identify the vital role played by the change agents. Revealing that the unique way in which the change agents became infused into the local community had a significant impact on fostering mutual trust that led to successful Internet adoption. Furthermore, we demonstrate that the provision of customized training programs by the change agents was a critical success factor. Finally, we reflect on the successful diffusion projects and identify the characteristics of the change agents that were instrumental in ensuring Internet adoption.

---

micro-businesses, information technology, Internet adoption and diffusion, change agents

---

Correspondence and requests for reprints should be sent to Pascale de Berranger, The Business School, Department of Business Information Technology, Manchester Metropolitan University, Aytoun Building, Aytoun Street, Manchester, England, M1 3GH. E-mail: P.Deberranger@mmu.ac.uk

[1]*Micro-business* is defined here as having 10 or less employees.

1. INTRODUCTION

Nooteboom [1] alerted us to the fact that small businesses play as critical a role as large businesses in the world economies. Statistics from the Department of Trade and Industry in the United Kingdom (UK) confirm the importance of small and medium-sized enterprises (SMEs) to the British economy [2]. Collectively, they are responsible for 65% of employment and 57% of gross domestic product [3]. SMEs are often able to gain an advantage over their larger competitors through their ability to be more responsive to new market opportunities. This is especially true in creative industries, such as music and art, where continuous innovation is crucial. Many SMEs, however, do not possess the full range of physical or intellectual resources with which to implement and utilize information and communication technologies (ICTs) to its full potential. This is a major inhibitor of Internet adoption and diffusion within SMEs.

There is a growing recognition by policy makers in Europe that the creative sector is expanding [4–6]. Although there is awareness that dynamic creative micro-businesses are vital to European global competitiveness, academic research into ICT diffusion in the creative sector is scarce with few published studies to date [7]. At a European level, the cultural sector is taken to encompass heritage, literature, the press, music, the performing arts, visual and audio–visual media, and sociocultural activities [8]. O'Brien and Feist [4] explained this surge of interest in the following terms:

> In the past, careers in the Arts were seen as risky but as employment in non-arts fields becomes less certain, the relative risk associated with arts employment will continue to decline and we are likely to see an increase in the number of people entering the sector. (p. 37)

This situation prompted the European Union to finance a number of initiatives through its Adapt and European Social funds. One of these initiatives is the Northern Quarter Network project (NQN), which also benefitted from additional support by the UK government through its Single Regeneration Budget. The Northern Quarter is a commercial region of Manchester—the third largest city in England. Historically, the area was a manufacturing center but is currently being regenerated and is home to numerous small creative businesses [9]. The NQN project was led by the Manchester Institute of Popular Culture, which is part of the Manchester Metropolitan University. The project lasted for 2 years and ended in January 1998. Its premise was diverse. The area concerned in this research was the provision of support and development opportunities for small and micro-businesses in the creative industries. This was based on recognition by the Manchester Institute of Popular Culture of the lack of business skills and information and communication technologies development within this sector. There was a strong training element to the project, involving practices based on a reactive as opposed to prescribed training processes [10]. The focus of this article is on creative micro-businesses that have a strong presence in the Northern Quarter. Through interviews with key stakeholders, we identify change agent characteristics as a critical success factor in the technology diffusion process in creative industries.

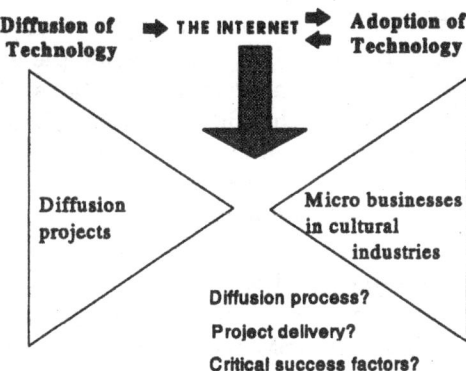

Figure 1. Northern Quarter Network project research in context.

The interface between diffusion projects and potential ICTs adopters is depicted in Figure 1. It is at this interface where the encounter between change agents and first-line adopters occurs. Rogers's [11] theory underpins much of the current diffusion and adoption literature. It defines change agents as "individuals who influence clients' innovation decisions in a direction deemed desirable by a change agency" (p. 6). A *change agency* is the body responsible for diffusion projects—the Manchester Institute of Popular Culture in this case. *First-line* adopters are those organizations that initially adopt an innovation within a given group or cluster of individuals or companies.

In this article we examine the NQN project using Rogers's [11] Innovation Diffusion Process (IDP) model as an analytical framework. It shows how the change agents effectively utilized existing informal communication channels to provide context-specific information. This information was customized with due regard to the specific circumstances faced by individual businesses and was thus of immediate practical value. Furthermore, this research identifies that the provision of customized training programs, delivered only as required to individual businesses, was a re-enforcing factor. The article concludes by offering fruitful areas of future research.

2. LITERATURE REVIEW

Most models and methodologies related to ICT diffusion and adoption are based on data collected in large organizations and may not be directly applicable to micro-businesses [12]. Research into large organizations tends to focus on formally documented processes. Micro-businesses, however, tend to lack such evidence due to the informality inherent in their size. This creates a need for distinct modes of inquiry that focus on informal business processes. Despite the substantial amount of literature published on SMEs (e.g., see [13–18]), there is a scarcity of literature specifically related to micro-businesses. Creative industries are particularly neglected. Similarly, although there are many papers published on technology diffusion, none was found to relate specifically to creative micro-businesses.

SMEs are often considered flexible enterprises [19]. Some research suggests that such flexibility will make ICT adoption relatively simple to achieve [20, 21] and that a greater speed of adoption than larger organizations might be expected [22]. These assertions appear to ignore the difficulties brought about by lack of time, cash flow issues, lack of expertise, and limited knowledge of the technology, all of which typify micro-businesses [17]. Communication issues between technology diffusers and first-line adopters are similarly neglected. From the technology supply side, there is a bewildering variety of information sources. Furthermore, the use of technical jargon and the rapid pace of technological advancement serve to increase the level of complexity and uncertainty faced by micro-businesses [23–25]. The literature clearly indicates that SMEs use ICTs primarily for routine, administrative, and operational purposes [13, 20, 26]. ICT is not generally perceived as a strategic resource [26].

Rogers's [11] model deconstructs the diffusion and adoption process into components allowing for a deeper scrutiny of each constituent part. Furthermore, Rogers's framework is extremely comprehensive, having been refined and extended over a number of years (e.g., see [27]) and provides a useful basis for examination. The model itself was not developed specifically for use within micro-businesses. Consequently, this research provides an exploratory application within the Northern Quarter. It aims to show that the change agents were able to use the informal communication channels that were inherent in the Northern Quarter to positively influence emerging perceptions of the Internet, thereby leading to successful adoption. More recent research focusing on ICT suggests that the traditional IDP model may be insufficient to explain the diffusion process for technologies that have an interorganizational focus [28]. It is suggested that economic and critical mass theories contribute to an understanding of diffusion in this context [28]. Clearly, the Internet falls into the category of an interorganizational technology; hence, this research has been undertaken with an appreciation that at this time, business use of the Internet is approaching critical mass and that electronic commerce (e-commerce) is viable for micro-businesses. One of the many examples confirming this is of a small UK telecommunications company that is using the Internet to compete successfully with larger rivals [28]. This research is set in context in Figure 2.

Diffusion is seen by Rogers as a "special type of communication" [10]. Because what is being diffused is new to potential adopters, this newness (of the ideas, processes, or objects) means that there is a high level of uncertainty involved. One important theme supported by both Attewell [29] and Rogers [11] is that information is one of the main means of reducing uncertainty. Agarwal and Prasad [30] found that communication channels are critical to facilitating innovation adoption. Their study looks at the effects of two communication channels—interpersonal and mass media—for the development of perceptions. They found that, "although the importance of interpersonal channels has been widely acknowledged in the literature, mass media channels also have a key role to play" (p. 27). The Internet has been widely publicized in the mass media, but it is questionable whether this alone is enough for uncertainty to diminish sufficiently to lead to adoption by micro-businesses in creative industries. The importance of interpersonal communication to the diffusion process is investigated in this article. In this regard, the role of change agents should not be underestimated. Attewell [29] emphasized the role of

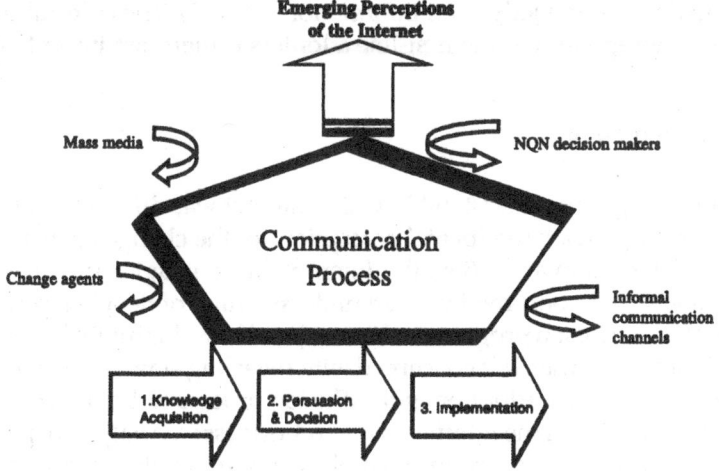

Figure 2. Stages in the innovation adoption process (adapted from Rogers [11]).

"knowledge providers" whose responsibility it is to lower the knowledge deficiencies of potential ICT adopters.

Rogers [11] identified a number of factors in change agents' success. A number of these were observed in the NQN project:

- *Effort in contacting clients:* Effort in the context of diffusion relates to the amount of interpersonal communication with clients.
- *Contact timing:* Participants in the NQN project had already gained sufficient understanding of the Internet through mass media communication. This had generated a propensity to adopt the technology.
- *Orientation:* Client-orientated change agents are inclined to have a close relationship and serious credibility in the eyes of their clients. Consequently, they are predisposed to basing their diffusion efforts on individual clients' needs.
- *Compatibility with client's needs:* Knowledge of clients' attitudes, beliefs, and social norms is necessary if the change processes are to be molded to clients' needs.
- *Level of empathy with clients:* Rogers [11] hypothesized that although there is very little empirical support for this expectation, change agent success is positively related to empathy with clients.

In addition, Rogers [11] introduced the notion of information overload in relation to the large volume of information flow in the diffusion exercise. He recognized that, "by understanding the needs and problems of his or her clients, a change agent can selectively transmit to them only information that is relevant" (p. 315).

The importance of interpersonal networks in the adoption or rejection of an innovation has been highlighted. Similarly, it has been recognized that the diffusion of innovation is frequently a social as well as a technical process [11]. Lee [31] proposed that, "beyond the issue of competition, firms and organisations also have their own sense of the world around them, or culture, which inhibits (or promotes) the sharing of new knowledge and information" (p. 152). The cultural compatibility of the change agents and the first-line adopters is therefore important.

3. METHODOLOGY

This research sought to understand how the Internet was diffused to and adopted by project participants. Participants' perceptions of the change agents, the project delivery, and the innovation (i.e., the Internet) were sought. In epistemological terms, the research is concerned with an understanding of people's perceptions or world view (of a diffusion program in this case) and how this might have influenced them to adopt the Internet. It is concerned with revealing similarities in perceptions at different stages of the adoption and diffusion process to isolate critical success factors to the adoption of the Internet in micro-businesses. Analysis of people's perceptions is interpretative in essence, emphasizing understanding as opposed to confirmation [32]. Consequently, the research approach was to undertake in-depth, semistructured interviews with the owner managers of the SMEs in the Northern Quarter. The sampling criteria for SMEs were as follows:

1. Interviewee had to work for a micro-business in the creative industry.
2. His/her organization had to have participated in the NQN project and have a Web site.
3. He/she had to have been instrumental in the decision to adopt the innovation.
4. The organization had to employ more than one person (i.e., sole proprietors and individuals trading as sole employee through limited organizations were not included as they were not considered to form a "company").

The NQN project involved a total of 15 companies, of which 8 agreed to be interviewed. The project owners provided a list of companies that fitted the sampling criteria (a number of companies did not fit criteria Number 4). They also provided contact names. As is always the case in this type of project, an audit trail was kept and is available for scrutiny by funding agencies. The audit trail includes names and contact information of participating companies, written agreements to take part in the project, and cost breakdown overall. Change agents deliberately kept the amount of red tape to a minimum to fit in with the informal style of small and micro-creative businesses in the Northern Quarter.

It appeared, at the negotiation stage, that both parties (change agents and participants) had developed friendly relationships with one another. It was felt that this might hinder respondents' honesty, as a large part of the areas of interest were concerned with how the project had been managed and the training delivered. To counteract this as much as possible, assurance of confidentiality was given. The interviewer also explained that the research was carried out with the change agents' full knowledge and that both the researcher and the change agents were keen to record a true picture of the process. Changes were also made to the contacts originally provided. In two cases, it appeared that the person named on the list had not been directly involved in the project. In both cases, the individual whose decision, power, and involvement had been instrumental in adoption was approached and interviewed.

All interviews were conducted by the same researcher. The researcher had no previous involvement in the project and had no contact with either the change agency or the change agents up to that point. Although interviews followed an agenda, they were left open so that comments and answers could open up the interview itself—an "emergent approach." The first part of the interview was structured and quantitative in essence. The idea was to gather information on companies and the interviewees, which would provide an overview of what the sample was physically made of. The following information was sought:

- Organizations' background (purpose, years of trading, number of employees, use of information technology [IT], etc.)
- Informants' background (job title, education, etc.)
- Informants use and knowledge of IT before the project

This data was used to give a background to the project participants. The second part was semistructured and covered four distinct areas:

- The use and perception of IT, including the Internet prior to and after the project
- The project, the project workers or change agents' approach, and the learning experience
- The Northern Quarter
- Government initiatives

3.1 Data Analysis

A grounded theory approach to data analysis was chosen based on Strauss and Corbin's [33] methodology. Interview transcripts were read and key data extracted using Rogers's [11] IDP (modified) model as an interpretative framework. This model divides the adoption process into three distinct stages:

- Knowledge acquisition, which relates to participants knowledge of the innovation prior to having knowledge of the project
- Persuasion and decision, which is associated with the adoption process
- Implementation, which concentrates on post adoption and use of the innovation after the project ended

The responses from the NQN project participants were then classified within each of the three stages:

- Knowledge acquisition
  1. The Internet
  2. Other initiatives
  3. The Northern Quarter

- Persuasion and decision
  1. Change agents' infusion method
  2. Characteristics of change agents
  3. Training and support
  4. Reasons for joining the project

- Implementation
  1. Companies' Web site
  2. Benefits of the project

Following this analysis framework, each interview resulted in a cognitive map to reveal informants' perceptions of the Internet adoption process and to highlight factors they believed were enabling and constraining that process. Maps were organized according to Roger's [11] modified framework. Cognitive maps for our purpose serve as a visuospatial representation of the structure and content of an individual's belief system [34]. They do not, as is often the case, show cause and effect. Those maps were then consolidated into a textual analysis that was in turn distilled and translated to form a composite map (Figure 3). Translation was necessary to present the findings in terms understandable to academic readers. This composite map forms the basis for the discussion presented in this article.

It has been argued that cognitive map building involves looking at what has gone on before that might affect beliefs about the present and the future. Eden [35] warned

TRANSLATED COMPOSITE MAP

Knowledge Acquisition	Persuasion & decision	Implementation
THE INTERNET ➤ Perceived need to be on the Internet ➤ Clear intention to adopt ➤ Lack of knowledge of both the technology itself and its uses for business ➤ Certain level of uncertainty and in some cases fear **OTHER INITIATIVES** *GENERAL* ➤ Poor opinion in general ➤ Unclear aims and objectives ➤ Poor value for money/effort ➤ Perceived lack of support ➤ Lack of understanding of the nature of small businesses *PROJECT PROCESS* ➤ Access difficulties ➤ Importance of location ➤ Training content level ➤ Selection criteria **NORTHERN QUARTER** ➤ Strong affiliation to the area ➤ Dependence on the area for business survival and/or growth	**CHANGE AGENT INFUSION METHOD** ➤ Attendance/involvement at local events/activities ➤ Attendance/involvement at industry specific events ➤ Reliance of local social communication network for information dissemination ➤ Reliance on third part introduction **CHARACTERISTICS OF CHANGE AGENTS** ➤ Understanding of SBs priorities ➤ Office in the NQ ➤ An exchange, not a hand out ➤ Knowledge of individual businesses ➤ Knowledge of relevant industries **TRAINING/SUPPORT** ➤ Provide guidance ➤ Flexibility, adaptability and availability ➤ Collaboration and dialogue ➤ Provide technical knowledge as and when required ➤ Information provided in context ➤ Distinct roles **REASONS FOR JOINING THE PROJECT** ➤ Confidence that "these people" understood company's ethos and would communicate it in the right way ➤ Belief that project workers understood what the NQ was about ➤ Belief that project would not damage company's image ➤ Free training ➤ Free web site	**COMPANIES' WEBSITES** ➤ It made us money in the sense that the word spread, people heard about us ➤ The web makes things more equal between large and small companies ➤ It is an advert for the gallery ➤ It is helping the company profile wise around the world **BENEFITS OF THE PROJECT** ➤ Increased local and global communication ➤ Greater understanding of the technology thus leading to reduced level on uncertainty ➤ Increased prestige ➤ Increased cohesion and economic viability of the whole area

Figure 3. Composite map.

that this can be a problem if cognitive maps are used as a predictive tool when the basis of their content is elements of thinking at a given time. Such problems may be avoided if a weaker view of cognitive mapping is adopted [35]. Indeed, in this research, maps were used as a means of representing the data contained in interviews in a meaningful way. They were not used as a way to provide a faithful representation of respondents' reality but as an analysis and validation tool.

The use of an interpretative framework for data analysis is generally associated with a phenomenological approach, a view that interpretation of meaning is subjective [36]. This creates a number of issues regarding the validity and translation of the data and the transferability of the research findings. To ensure that data translation was faithful, the participants were asked to validate the translation through the medium of cognitive maps.

This study concentrated on the views of those businesses that went ahead with the project. The findings therefore present the views of adopters. Views of nonadopters will need to be sought in further research to provide a more complete picture of technology adoption in small creative businesses.

4. FINDINGS AND DISCUSSIONS

The following paragraph gives an overview of the interviewees, their position, and the level of IT knowledge and usage within their organization.

4.1 Background

All interviewees were in senior positions ranging from area managers to directors, partners, or managing directors. All had been educated to a higher education level. Participants classified their knowledge of IT from fair to poor. All companies but one had a computer on their premises, but none had Internet access. Usage of IT varied from no usage at all to basic word processing. Most of the word processing was used for writing letters to customers and generating listings for advertising purposes. It is interesting to note that the company that had a computer but did not use it had the most ideas on how to maximize efficiency through IT.

In conclusion, we can say that participants had a low level of IT knowledge and that usage was minimal and only included routine administrative tasks. This concurs with the findings of previous research [13, 20, 26]. This is important in the context of the NQN project. Participating organizations were very small businesses with little IT knowledge and time to spare. Internet adoption, or in this case the construction and design of a Web site, was a big step for these small companies and was viewed by them as a difficult process.

This research has identified the vital importance of change agents in influencing the diffusion process from first point of contact to actual adoption of the technology. Findings related to the persuasion and decision stage is summarized in Figure 4.

At the start of the NQN project, participants already possessed a propensity to adopt the Internet but were constrained by their lack of knowledge and resources. The change agents wereZ instrumental in moving them successfully to the implementation stage. Their obvious enthusiasm for the project and their belief in the viability of the project were essential prerequisites to its success.

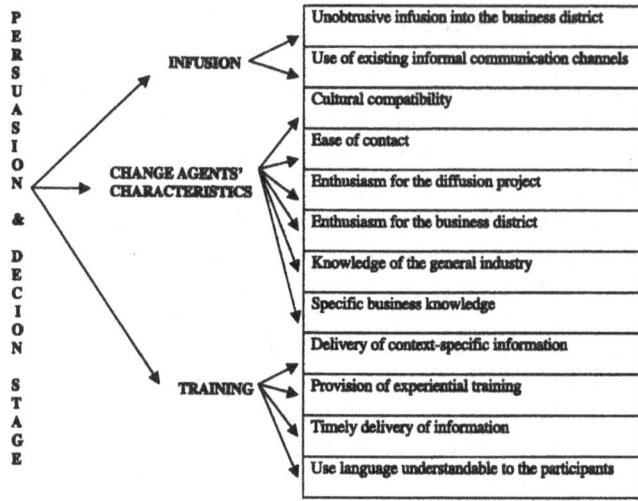

Figure 4. Characteristics of change agents as critical success factors in the innovation diffusion process.

4.2 Infusion Process

4.2.1 Trust Issues. Surveys in the past have shown that micro-businesses tend to harbor distrust of government initiatives [36–38]. Reasons for this were identified by project participants in the Northern Quarter as

- Unclear aims and objectives
- Lack of support
- Poor value for money or efforts
- Lack of understanding of the nature of and constraints experienced by micro-businesses

Through mass media communications, participants were aware that strategic benefits were generally attributed to the Internet. A respondent explained that the problems associated with Internet adoption stem from their lack of trust in IT professionals: "IT professional are like garages and mechanics, people are afraid of putting their car in because they don't understand." This concurs with Rogers's [11] view that lack of knowledge and the resulting lack of trust is a major inhibitor of diffusion. Therefore, a combination of the high uncertainty associated with mass media communications, a general mistrust of diffusion initiatives, and a lack of organizational resources had previously inhibited the adoption process. The subtle manner in which the change agents infused themselves into the NQN played a significant part in engendering the atmosphere of mutual trust, which underpinned the project.

4.2.2 Informal Communication Network. In the NQN project, the change agents made a conscious decision to become gradually infused into the local social system. They then relied on knowledge dissemination of the project by word of mouth. This was achieved by utilization of the existing informal communication networks and by introductions through third parties. This approach had the dual advantage of saving money on advertising and, more important, fostering trust. The information about the project "filtered down" existing communication networks. In this way, the project appeared more plausible to the participants than if it had been advertised in the mass media. Rogers [11] highlighted how social systems could either hinder or improve the diffusion process. In the NQN, the unobtrusive approach used by the change agents was fundamental in allaying suspicions. Reliance on local communication networks was only possible because the change agents had been involved in local activities and attended industry-specific events. In this way, they had become accepted into the local social system prior to the start of the project. The findings thus agree with both Hackney et al.'s [39] and Charlton et al.'s [40] views that successful infiltration of the population of interest must rely on the identification and use of existing informal social networks. The research results are also in accordance with Meyer and Goes [41] who explained that micro-businesses rely on informal communication networks as a means to increase information quality. As one respondent explained, "there was no advertising, we just heard and that helped." However, it should be noted that this may only be possible when the target population is clustered in close geographical proximity.

4.2.3 Effort. Rogers [11] stated that one of the factors that positively influenced change agents' success was the amount of effort expended in contacting clients. This research found that the effort expanded by the change agents at all stages of the NQN project was considerable and had a significant influence on its success. One interviewee explained that she needed to be sure that the change agents were committed to the project and added that she would otherwise not have gotten involved. Interviewees stated that they joined the project because they were confident that the change agents understood what their company stood for. Therefore, it appears that business image is an issue. The importance of image for micro-businesses in the creative industries would appear to be specifically (but not only) related to Internet adoption. This is a reflection of the Internet's position as an outward-facing, multimedia technology thus being of considerable influence in image projection. There was no mention of this in the Internet adoption literature surveyed.

4.2.4 Empathy. Despite empirical evidence, Rogers [11] surmised that the level of change agent empathy with clients is positively related to successful technology adoption. Interview data collected during this research suggests that empathy relates to a strong commitment to the project; commitment to the success of each organization's Web site; being involved in companies' problems and activities; and most important, being based in and having an understanding of the aspirations of the businesses in the Northern Quarter. The level of commitment, local presence, and local involvement of the change agents increased the level of perceived empathy of the micro-businesses. Physical presence also facilitated ease of access to the change agents. This was compatible with the provision of a customized and flexible training program as described later.

4.3 Strategic Benefits

All interviewees showed a strong awareness of the benefits of using the Internet, but they had doubts, fears or uncertainties about it. These were based on either lack of knowledge of the actual technology and its use, or on a general mistrust of the information provided via mass media. Nonetheless, they were all aware of the potential benefits of using the Internet and, more particularly, the usefulness of a presence on the Web. The following comments illustrate this point:

- "A web site is a publicity platform."
- "You can be here and do business with someone in LA."
- "It is going to become THE media, to become life."
- "You can have public relations and advertising but it is someone else's interpretation. With an Internet site it is more hands on, if you are not happy you can change it."
- "We wanted to be able to e-mail information as opposed to using fax or telephone. It would save us time and money."

4.4 Change Agents' Characteristics

The interviewees were asked to describe the specific characteristics of the change agents who were instrumental in their decision to adopt Internet technology. The agents were physically located in the Northern Quarter, which enabled considerable face-to-face contact. This "personal touch" was critical in building up the necessary trust between the change agents and the micro-businesses. Great importance was attached to the change agents' willingness to become involved within the Northern Quarter area and for their high level of enthusiasm for both the project and the Northern Quarter itself. Similarly, the agent's obvious understanding of creative business in general, and of the participating companies in particular, was very important. Indeed, most participants stated that they were very impressed by the fact the change agents had actually done their "homework" and knew what each specific business was about prior to first meeting participants. Meetings often took place in bars or pubs, which was mentioned as a "good thing." The informal yet professional attitude of the agents was seen to be in alignment with the internal culture of the businesses themselves. Respondents rated care toward and understanding of their business, care and enthusiasm about the project itself, and general attitude, as highly important.

4.5 Training Process

4.5.1 Flexible Delivery. Some of the problems associated with Internet adoption are directly linked with the characteristics of small businesses. One company explained that the problem with the Internet adoption is "getting it all set out while working flat out at the same time." This issue was common to all interviews where respondents point to a lack of time as a problem. Most respondents mentioned the need for flexibility in the training and support program to fit in with small business priorities.

It is interesting to note that all but one of those interviewed saw the project as a joint effort between the change agents and themselves rather than simply the provision of a service: "It all came together as a community working for the same cultural end in the same area." Participants expressed in the following terms how the change agents delivered training:

- "They were able to guide us."
- "It was a real process of dialogue."
- "We looked at different companies' web sites where as before it was just talking about web sites. That helped us understand the capabilities of the Internet ourselves and that obviously gave us ideas on where to take our sites."
- "We said what we wanted and they explained the implications of our wants."
- "We'd come up with an idea and they would explain how to interpret it in technical terms."

Just as critical was the agents' ability to provide information in an informal yet professional manner. The businesses themselves operated in a relaxed but efficient fashion. This is an example of the cultural compatibility that existed between the change agents and the participants.

4.5.2 Information Provision. The change agents provided context-specific information to each micro-business. This served two important purposes. First, the participants were better able to understand how the Internet could have benefits for their specific businesses. The change agents sought out Web sites from businesses in the same industry and explained the technical aspects of the Web pages without using technical jargon. They also explained how the sites were being used to generate additional business. For example, one business in the music industry was introduced to a Web site from a rival company. The change agent guided the owner through the site, explaining both the technical and business aspects in non-technical terms. This process was successful because of the mutual trust that had already been cultivated between the change agents and the micro-businesses. This served to increase the confidence of the participants in the Internet because they could see for themselves that the potential benefits were real. As one respondent stated, "Before it was just talking about it and not seeing it." The second purpose was the prevention of information overload. The participants were bombarded by so much information from the mass media that they were unable to absorb it or make rational judgements based on it. The change agents overcame this by filtering and presenting information that was relevant to a particular company in a specific set of circumstances (i.e., context specific). Furthermore, the information was delivered only at the time when it was needed. Therefore, each micro-business received a customized and flexible diffusion program relevant to their specific business circumstances and current level of knowledge.

Our research showed that mass media knowledge of the benefits of Internet adoption was not in itself sufficient to lead to adoption. Those interviewed felt the need for more experientially based knowledge before they could adopt Internet technology. The hands-on approach used by the change agents was a critical success factor in achieving this.

The literature reviewed showed that technical knowledge transfer is better suited to interpersonal communication channels [11, 29]. Attewell [29] added that it is the role of change agents to lower knowledge deficiencies of potential adopters. Both of these assertions were verified by interviewee's comments. They were aware of Internet technologies through mass media communication but needed context-specific technical knowledge to reduce uncertainty. Respondents relied on the change agents to fill the technical knowledge gaps. Rogers [11] and Attewell [29] both stressed the importance of technical knowledge at the adoption stage of diffusion. The findings suggest that technical knowledge was required earlier, at the decision stage of the adoption process.

4.6 Internet Adoption Benefits

Once the interviewees had made the decision to adopt Internet technology, they were asked what benefits they believed would accrue. These were reported as

- Access to local and international markets
- Direct selling
- Improved company profile
- The ability to train others
- Indirect financial benefits

These answers indicated that the interviewees now generally regarded the Internet as a strategic resource. This was a major change in perception from the start of the project. It shows the difference in perception from the general view about IT as an administrative and operational tool [13, 20, 26]. Benefits were also related to a better knowledge of the technology. This is a function of the training being tailored to the needs of participants as opposed to being set as a rigid agenda. All participants expressed increased confidence with the technology.

4.7 Actual Benefits

The degree to which participants integrated Internet technologies into their everyday business practices following the diffusion exercise was varied and fragmented. The benefits put forward for having adopted the technology are outlined in the following:

- Improved company profile
- Access to markets, local and international
- Direct selling
- Cost-effective advertising (through using both e-mail and having a presence on the Web)
- Increased communication locally and internationally
- Cost-effective communication (using e-mail)

5. CONCLUSIONS

Internet-based trading is often portrayed as a medium in which micro-businesses can compete on equal terms with large organizations. However, many micro-businesses struggle to develop and implement successful Web-based solutions. One possible reason for this is that insufficient attention is given to the role played by change agents in the diffusion and adoption process. Given that the number of people with Web access is increased exponentially, micro-businesses that do not exploit the new medium stand to suffer serious competitive disadvantages.

This article discussed the application of Roger's [11] IDP model within Manchester's NQN project. It was found that certain characteristics of the change agents amounted to critical success factors for the successful adoption of Internet technologies within creative micro-businesses in the United Kingdom. Specifically, it was observed that the change agents were most influential at the persuasion and decision stage of the innovation diffusion process. Through application of the IDP model within the NQN project, it has been possible to identify three areas within the persuasion and decision stage in which change agents had greatest influence. First, at the point of infusion, the change agents adopted an unobtrusive approach that utilized existing informal communication networks. At this time, the change agents were not known personally by the businesses in the NQN, and individuals had no reason to trust them. This infusion method increased trust in both the change agents and the diffusion initiative. Within the second area, the change agents' personal characteristics, such as enthusiasm and specific business knowledge, were indicators of a cultural compatibility between the change agents and the businesses. This was crucial in giving the businesses the confidence to proceed with Internet adoption. In addition, knowledge of micro-businesses characteristics and their respective industrial sector contributed to the change agents' success. Finally, the provision of customized training programs accelerated Internet implementation and provided a deeper understanding of the implications of Web sites in their specific industries.

The NQN project has provided a means of improving the viability of participating companies and has raised the profile of creative activities in Manchester. A strong affiliation to the area appears to have been a prerequisite to achieving this.

The Northern Quarter of Manchester has two important distinguishing features that influence the generalization to the research results. The first is cohesiveness. This is related to the geographical co-location of the businesses; the second is homogeneity. All the businesses were in creative industries and thus had similar organizational cultures. These distinguishing features may limit the extent to which the results of this research may be more widely applied. However, there are numerous examples of other districts within the United Kingdom that possess similar distinguishing features and for which this research has direct relevance. Other countries within the European community have similar districts such as Temple Bar in Dublin, Ireland; Poble Nou in Barcelona, Spain; and Veemarktkwaartier in Tillburg, The Netherlands. Furthermore, many of the change agent characteristics identified here are not dependent on the distinguishing features of the Northern Quarter and are more generally applicable to technology diffusion projects in micro-businesses.

6. FUTURE RESEARCH

Rogers [11] provided a useful framework for analyzing diffusion projects. This framework has been applied to the NQN project and has proved to be a valuable analytical tool. Research outcomes in the Northern Quarter were found to be generally supportive of Rogers's [11] theory. Further research is necessary to ascertain whether the findings of this research project can be generalized to micro-businesses in other industries and in other geographical regions. Research should also concentrate on classifying micro-businesses according to size and type of industries. This could highlight important cultural differences.

Both Rogers [11] and Attewell [29] stated that the importance of technical knowledge is relatively more important at the adoption stage of diffusion. The research findings suggest that, in the case of adoption through diffusion, technical knowledge is required at the decision stage. This warrants further investigation.

A major area of interest following directly from this research is encapsulated in the views and perceptions of small businesses that did not participate in the NQN project. Investigation of this group could reveal reasons for nonadoption and would further enlighten the debate in the context of technology diffusion. We intend to undertake this research.

It was also highlighted that building business image on the Internet was a major factor that influenced companies to participate in the project. This may be related to the organizational culture of the creative industries in which image projection is regarded as highly important. Further research in this area could investigate whether this also applies to other industrial sectors. The hypothesis to be tested would be that creative businesses are relatively more aware of the importance of their image than other industries. Therefore, an outward facing technology such as the Internet could have greater impact on company image.

As the trend toward globalization continues inexorably, cross-national and cross-cultural research into technology diffusion will become of prime importance. It is intended that this article should act as a catalyst to stimulate such research in countries other than the United Kingdom and hence to provide a fertile bedrock for future international collaborative projects in this field.

REFERENCES

[1] B. Nooteboom, "The facts about small business and the real values of its 'life world,'" *American Journal of Economics and Sociology*, vol. 47, no. 3, pp. 299–314, 1988.

[2] Department of Trade and Industry, *Small Firms in Britain Report*. London: Her Majesty's Stationery Office, 1995.

[3] D. Madsing, "NCC presentation on the information technology initiative," Invited presentation at Manchester Metropolitan University, England, 1997.

[4] J. O'Brien and A. Feist, "Employment in the arts and cultural industries: An analysis of the 91 census," Art Council of England, London, Research Rep. No. 2, 1995.

[5] W. Mathies, "Culture and structural policies: A contribution to employment," in *Initial Feasibility Study: Cultural Industries Support Services*, J. O'Connor, Ed. Manchester, England: Manchester Institute of Popular Culture, Manchester Metropolitan University, 1997.

[6] European Union, "Culture, the cultural industries and employment," *Commission Staff Working Paper SEC(98)837*, Part 3, Conclusions, (1998, May). Available: http://europa.eu.int/search97cgi/

[7] J. O'Connor and J. Ebrey, "Cultural production: Action research project—Review of existing research," Manchester Institute of Popular Culture, England, Mar. 1996.
[8] Policy Studies Institute, "Employment in the cultural sector," J. Eckstein (Ed.), *Cultural Trends*, vol. 5, no. 4, pp. 1–33, 1994.
[9] D. Hill, "The Northern Quarter Network," *Institute for Popular Culture*, Part 1–4, (1995, June). Available: http://es-www.mmu.ac.uk:81/cgi-bin/betsie/parser2.pl/www.mmu.ac.uk/h-ss/mipc/nqnrept1.htm
[10] J. O'Connor, "ESF adapt—Northern Quarter; Networking for business advantage," *Newsletter No. 1*, pp. 4, Nov.–Dec.1996.
[11] E. M. Rogers, *Diffusion of Innovation*. New York: Free Press, 1983.
[12] G. I. Doukidis, P. Lybereas, and R. D. Galliers, "Information system planning in small business: A stage of growth analysis," *Journal of Systems and Software*, vol. 33, no. 2, pp. 189–201, 1996.
[13] Irish Management Institute, "Microcomputers in the administration and management processes in smaller business: The emerging experience in EEC countries," *Commission of the European Communities*, 1992.
[14] J. N. Marshall, N. Alderman, C. Wong, and A. Thwaits, "The impact of government-assisted management training and development on small and medium-sized enterprises in Britain," *Environment and Planning C-Government and Policy*, vol. 11, no. 3, pp. 331–348, 1993.
[15] S. Blili and L. Raymond, "Information technology: Threats and opportunities for small and medium-sized enterprises," *International Journal of Information Management*, vol. 13, no. 6, pp. 439–448, 1993.
[16] J. Y. L. Thong and C. S. Yap, "CEO characteristics, organizational characteristics and information technology adoption in small businesses," *Omega: The International Journal of Management Science*, vol. 23, no. 4, pp. 429–442, 1995.
[17] C. S. Yap and J. Y. L. Thong, "Programme evaluation of a government information technology programme for small businesses," *Journal of Information Technology*, vol. 12, no. 2, pp. 107–120, 1997.
[18] J. Y. L. Thong, "An integrated model of information systems adoption in small businesses," *Journal of Management Information Systems*, vol. 15, no. 4, pp. 187–214, 1999.
[19] M. Levy and P. Powell, "SME flexibility and the role of information systems," *Small Business Economics*, vol. 11, pp.183–196, 1998.
[20] S. C. Malone, "Computerizing small business information systems," *Journal of Small Business Management*, pp. 10–16, April 1985.
[21] A. R. Montazemi, "Factors affecting information satisfaction in the context of the small business environment," *MIS Quarterly*, vol. 12, no. 2, pp. 238–256, Jun. 1988.
[22] D. J. Storey and R. Cressy, "Small business risk: A firm and bank perspective," in *Small Business Economics*, Vol. 11, *SME Flexibility and the Role of Information Systems*, M. Levy and P. Powell, Eds. Coventry, England: Warwick Business School SME Centre, 1998, p.183.
[23] E. Geisler, "Information technology department," *IEEE Trans. on Engineering Management*, vol. 39, no.2, pp. 112, 1992.
[24] E. Fuller, "Business development through IT adoption—A learning agenda," in Business and its Contribution to Regional and International Development, 39th ICSB World Conference 1993, J. J. Obrecht and M. Bayad, Eds. Strasbourg, Germany: Robert Schuman University, 1994, pp. 95–104.
[25] D. Tucker and P. de Berranger, "Nurturing trust and reactive training: Essential elements in ICT diffusion projects," presented at IRMA International Conference Proceedings, Anchorage, Alaska, 2000.
[26] Manchester Technology Management Centre, "The North West Regional Business Usage of Information and Communications Technology Survey," MTMC Manchester, Internal Report, 1997.
[27] T. H. Kwon and R. W. Zmud, "Unifying the fragmented models of information systems implementation," in *Critical Issues in Information Systems Research*, R. J. Boland and R. A. Hirschheim, Eds. New York: Wiley, 1987, pp. 227–251.
[28] M. B. Prescott and S. A. Conger, "Information technology innovations: A classification by IT locus of impact and research approach," *The DATABASE for Advances in Information Systems*, vol. 26, no. 2, pp. 20–41, 1995.
[29] P. Attewell, "Technology diffusion and organisational learning: The case of business computing," *Organization Science*, vol. 3, no. 1, pp.1–19, 1992.

[30] R. Agarwal and J. Prasad, "The antecedents and consequences of user perceptions in information technology adoption," *Decision Support Systems*, vol. 22, no. 1, pp.15–29, 1998.

[31] A. S. Lee, "Electronic mail as a medium for rich communication—An empirical investigation using hermeneutic interpretation," *MIS Quarterly*, vol. 18, no. 2, pp. 143–157, 1994.

[32] M. B. Miles and A. M. Huberman, *Qualitative Data Analysis*, 2nd ed. Thousand Oaks, CA: Sage, 1994.

[33] A. Strauss and J. Corbin (Eds.), *Grounded Theory in Practice*. London: Sage, 1997.

[34] P. S. Budhwar, "Cognitive mapping technique to study managerial cognitions: Methodology considered," Manchester Business School, England, Working Paper No. 339, March 1996.

[35] C. Eden, "Cognitive mapping," *European Journal of Operational Research*, vol. 36, no. 1, pp. 1–3, 1988.

[36] P. Lewis, *Information Systems Development*. London: Pitman, 1994.

[37] B. J. Harrer, R. O. Weijo, and M. P. Hattrup, "The role of change agents in new product adoption," *Industrial Marketing Management*, vol. 17, no. 2, pp. 95–102, 1988.

[38] G. Bannock, "Choking the spirit of enterprise," *International Management*, vol. 37, pp. 30–33, Mar. 1992.

[39] R. Hackney, J. Kawalek, and G. Dhillon, "Information technology & communication management within SMEs: Opportunities for partnership," presented at the UKAIS Conf., Southampton University, England, 1996.

[40] C. Charlton, C. Gittings, P. Leng, J. Little, and I. Neilson, "Diffusion of the Internet: A local perspective on an international issue," in *Facilitating Technology Transfer Through Partnership, Learning from Practice and Research*, T. McMaster, E. Mumford, E. B. Swanson, B. Warboys, and D. Wastell, Eds. London: Chapman & Hall, 1997, pp. 337–354.

[41] O. Meyers and J. B. Goes, "How organizations adopt and implement new technologies," *Academy of Mangagement Proceedings*, pp. 175–179, 1987.

Journal of Organizational Computing and Electronic Commerce

Instructions for Contributors

The *Journal of Organizational Computing and Electronic Commerce* publishes original research articles concerned with impacts of computer and communication technology on organizational design, operations, and performance. It serves as a forum for stimulating and disseminating research into the implications of these technologies for organizational structure and dynamics, the technological advances needed to keep pace with organizational changes, and emerging technological possibilities for improving organizational productivity. The journal's focus is not on computing as it relates to individuals. Theoretical, experimental, and survey research are all appropriate to the *Journal of Organizational Computing and Electronic Commerce*. The journal's major editorial areas are computer-supported cooperative work (CSCW), group-ware, computer modeling of computer-aided coordination and organizational learning, economics of organizational computing, and behavioral studies of organizational computing. The refereeing of papers in each of these areas is directed by an Associate Editor. The journal also publishes relevant book reviews, meeting announcements, brief notes, and software reviews.

Manuscript Submission. Submit four manuscript copies to the Editor, Dr. Andrew B. Whinston, Department of Management Science and Information Systems, College and Graduate School of Business, University of Texas, Austin, TX 78712–1175. Articles should be concise and in English, not more than 40 pages and/or 12,000 words. This limitation applies to the entire paper—cover page, abstract, narrative, footnotes, figures, and references included. Manuscripts (including title page, abstract, text, quotes, acknowledgments, references, appendixes, tables, figure captions, and footnotes) should be typewritten, double-spaced, with one-inch margins on all sides, using 8½" × 11" paper, one side only. Each page of the manuscript should be numbered, starting with the title page. The title page should contain the article title, author(s), affiliations, a short form of the title (less than 55 characters including letters and spaces), and the name, complete mailing address, and telephone number of the author to whom correspondence should be sent. Page 2 should contain a short abstract (200–250 words) and 5–10 relevant key words. All acronyms should be spelled out where first used. Each table and figure must be submitted separately from the text; they must be referred to within the text but not be included within the text matter. Original illustrations (black and white only) must be legible after reduction to a maximum size of 5" × 8".

Style. The style guidelines of *Information for IEEE Transactions, Journals and Letters Authors* (1997 revision; available from IEEE Periodicals, Transactions/Journals Department, 455 Hoes Lane, Piscataway, NJ 08855) should be followed, especially for reference lists and text citation of sources. References should be in complete, IEEE-formatted, numbered reference list that is arranged in the order of citations in text, not in alphabetical order. In-text reference numbers should appear in square brackets. Make sure that the reference list citations correspond exactly with the in-text citations. Pages 4 through 5 of the style guide provide (a) detailed instructions on preparing references and citations and (b) sample references and citations. Articles in other styles can be submitted for review and if accepted for publication must be revised by the author.

Permissions. Authors are responsible for all statements made in their work and for obtaining permission from copyright owners to reprint or adapt a table or figure or to reprint a lengthy quotation of 500 words or more. Write to original author(s) and publisher to request nonexclusive world rights in all languages to use the material in the article and in future editions. Provide copies of all permissions and credit lines obtained.

Production Notes. Accepted manuscripts are copyedited, authors review copyediting, and manuscripts are typeset into page proofs. Authors are asked to read proofs for typesetter's errors and other defects. Correction of typographical errors is made without charge; other alterations are to be prepaid by authors. Authors may order reprints of their articles only when they return page proofs.